FACET fb BOOKS

BIBLICAL SERIES—20

John Reumann, General Editor

The Spirit-Paraclete
in the
Fourth Gospel

by HANS WINDISCH

translated by James W. Cox

FORTRESS PRESS   PHILADELPHIA

"The Five Johannine Paraclete Sayings" is a translation of "Die fünf johanneischen Parakletsprüche," first published in *Festgabe für Adolf Jülicher* (Tübingen: J. C. B. Mohr [Paul Siebeck], 1927), and is printed here by arrangement with the publisher.

"Jesus and the Spirit in the Gospel of John" is a translation of "Jesus und der Geist im Johannesevangelium," first published in *Amicitiae Corolla* (University of London Press, 1933), and is printed here by arrangement with the publisher.

5712I67   Printed in U.S.A.   1-3046

Introduction

HANS Windisch (1881-1935) was one of the last of the great New Testament scholars of the Liberal era in Germany, an interpreter who was not so much concerned with the theological side of Scripture or its meaning for the church of the day as he was with the meaning of a passage for its original readers and in light of the history-of-religions approach. His two essays on the sayings about the "Paraclete" in the Gospel of John, published in 1927 and 1933, still provide an important literary analysis of the verses, in spite of more than thirty years of subsequent study and recently discovered materials like the Dead Sea Scrolls.

Windisch was born at Leipzig on April 25, 1881, and after studies at the university there began a career of teaching in faculties of Protestant theology. Beginning as Privatdozent in New Testament at Leipzig in 1908, by 1914 he had been named professor of New Testament and early Christian literature at the University of Leiden, Holland. In 1929 he was called to a similar chair at the university at Kiel, Germany. Six years later he succeeded the renowned Ernst von Dobschütz as professor at Halle-Wittenberg, but in the fall of the year in which he entered that post he died following a lecture, on November 8, 1935, at the age of fifty-four, his work cut short in the prime of his career.

His comparatively brief career was marked, however, by great literary production. Windisch wrote commentaries in major German series on the Catholic epistles (1911, revised 1930), Hebrews (1913, revised 1931), *Barnabas* (1920), and II Corinthians (1924). He was the author of countless articles for learned journals, as well as of eight essays for *Festschriften,* and of articles for the German encyclopedia *Die Religion in Geschichte und Gegenwart.* Major books from his pen dealt with baptism and sin in primitive Christianity (1908), the "messianic war" and primitive Christianity (1909), Philo's piety (1909), John and the Synoptics (1926), Paul and Christ (1934), and Paul and Judaism (1935). The only one of his books to be translated into English was *The Meaning of the Sermon on the Mount.* In addition to writing and teaching, from 1912 until his death Windisch edited the series "Untersuchungen zum Neuen Testament."

Several features in Windisch's career were unusual in his day. The fact that he taught in Holland for fifteen of his most active years (1914-29) meant that during World War I he was able, in a neutral country, to continue his research and overseas contacts at a time when many German scholars were comparatively isolated. It also meant that some of his publications appeared in Dutch. Above all, it meant that Windisch read widely in the Anglo-Saxon literature on the New Testament and was himself known in England and America. (One of the essays here translated appeared in a volume in honor of a Quaker scholar in England, Rendel Harris.) To aid in restoring scholarly communication after the war he wrote for a German periodical a survey report covering English and American New Testament production from 1914 to 1920, while for the *Harvard Theological Review* he wrote two articles reporting on continental scholarship. He urged German colleagues to take cognizance of the intensive work being done in the Anglo-Saxon world. These reviews reflect broad reading. He singled out as significant, books such as those of J. H. Moulton and A. T. Robertson in Greek grammar, Henry Cadbury on Lucan language, Isaac Abrahams on Pharisaism, and Rendel Harris' work on "testimony literature."

Another fact of interest is that, upon assuming his chair at Halle, Windisch was also named to succeed von Dobschütz as editor of the "Corpus Hellenisticum." This undertaking aimed at producing a collection of parallels to New Testament words, terms, and passages from the literature of the Hellenistic world similar to that provided by J. J. Wettstein in his New Testament edition of 1751-52. Windisch inherited a plan and a file of countless slips with classical references on them, but his premature death caused the project to languish again, and only in recent years has the work once more been set in motion—interestingly enough now in Holland, where Windisch once taught (see W. C. van Unnik, "Corpus Hellenisticum Novi Testamenti," *Journal of Biblical Literature,* 83 [1964], pp. 17-33). Also worthy of note is the fact that, at his death, Windisch left several articles so complete that they could be published posthumously, as well as a revision of his book on the Sermon on the Mount, which Martin Dibelius saw through the press. It is probably fair to say, however, that the name of Windisch is not so widely known to subsequent decades of New Testament study as it deserves to be.

In part this relative neglect of Windisch obtains because times changed between his formative and his mature years, and trends then developing became even more pronounced after his death. Windisch was a product of the Liberal period. He identified himself with the *religionsgeschichtliche Schule* ("history-of-religions school"), which believed that Christianity was to be studied as just another of the world's religions, without any special presuppositions concerning "revelation" or "uniqueness." He was conscious of inheriting the results of critical study by such giants as Wilhelm Bousset, William Wrede, and Johannes Weiss, or—to mention scholars in whose honor he wrote essays —Adolf Harnack, Georg Heinrici, Wilhelm Herrmann, and Hermann Gunkel. All this meant that Windisch pursued a method which tried to keep itself free from dogma, church, and philosophical or doctrinal commitment, and sought "objective" results by use of philology, historical method, comparative religions, and archeology. In the "Introduction" to his book *The Meaning of the Sermon on the Mount*— and it is there (pp. 15-19) and in the section on "Theological Exegesis" (pp. 154 ff.) in the same book that the English reader should turn for a presentation of his views—Windisch notes that in addition to this emphasis on scientific study, New Testament scholarship had also taken another and different direction since 1918: that of theological interpretation. He singles out books by Dibelius, Rudolf Bultmann, and Ernst Lohmeyer as examples, but, above all, he has in mind the influence of Karl Barth's commentary on Romans (1919) as decisive for this new direction. He deplored this development and comments once that Barth's treatment of Romans 13 is "perhaps the worst example of exegetical mayhem" (p. 161, n. 4).

Thus Windisch championed "historical exegesis" and the resulting study of biblical *religion,* as over against "theological exegesis" and the resulting biblical *theology* with its concern for God, Christ, and "today" (relevance). Windisch was quite content to deal only with the meaning "then," for the original hearers. (One need not even be a Christian to make a contribution here.) Only after such work is done may the theologian go on to make further interpretations (and here the exegete ought to be one who shares in "the life of faith to which the New Testament witnesses," p. 156) but such was not the task of the "science of religion."

By turning to pages 167-213 of his book on the Sermon on the Mount, readers can see for themselves what sort of treatment resulted. Windisch treated Matthew 5-7 as a document by itself, not as part of "the total New Testament witness" or even in the full context of Jesus' preaching and teaching. (Actually Windisch divided Jesus' teaching into a "Galilean Gospel," including the Sermon and the Lord's Prayer, and a seemingly unrelated "Jerusalem Gospel" which spoke of his atoning death.) Emphasized above all was that this Sermon must not be read through Pauline glasses. Paul might think the demands of the Law unfulfillable, serving only to show man his need for a Savior. Windisch regarded the Sermon as something to be obeyed, as the way to righteousness. This position brought him into a sharp exchange of opinions with Bultmann, who asked, in a review, Who ever fulfilled the Sermon on the Mount? Does Windisch claim he did? The two also tangled over the imperatives in the Pauline epistles. In an article published in 1924, Bultmann argued that the Pauline imperatives (e.g., in Rom. 12-14) unfold out of the prior indicative statement about what God has done (Rom. 3, God has justified him who has faith). Windisch replied in the same year and in the same journal, arguing that Paul regarded himself (and all "normal" Christians) as free from sin; the imperatives are a leftover from ethically colored baptismal preaching. If there are contradictions in Paul, it is not the job of the scientist in religion to straighten them out. Paul scarcely needs Barth or Bultmann to give him lectures!

The fact is, however, that Barth and Bultmann became the significant voices in theology and New Testament study in the thirties and the following decades. The Liberal position was eclipsed—eventually even in America. This, coupled with his own premature death, meant that Windisch and his views had little influence, in spite of his great learning. Now, however, there are signs that a new era more appreciative of his method and work is at hand. The "history-of-religions" approach is being given a new hearing, though with presuppositions different from those held earlier in the century. The variety that Windisch stressed is again being emphasized over against unity. There is an effort to separate "historical" and "theological" (cf. Stendahl's "what it meant" and "what it means" in the article on "Biblical Theology, Contemporary," in *The Interpreter's Dictionary of the Bible* [New York and Nashville: Abingdon, 1962], Vol. 1, pp. 418-32)—even though some practitioners of this method do not necessarily want to endorse the notion that purely "objective" study is possible. (Windisch, as we shall see, was quite aware at times that subjective factors are present in interpretation, but in "modernizing" Jesus he felt he was doing something akin to what Paul or John had done: revising the sources in order to construct one's own picture of Jesus, under the impetus of the Spirit.) Windisch thus provides an excellent illustration of the strengths and weaknesses of the Liberal period—a type of scholarship still too little known today.

Two recent articles provide analyses of his work, the one a general account published originally in Sweden; and the other by a Roman Catholic expert, on Windisch's views about the meaning of Christ in the history-of-religions approach. The latter was a topic on which Windisch wrote several times, in more popular terms on the "historical Jesus" in 1910 and 1911, refuting the then current notion of the "Christ-myth" school that Jesus never lived, and again in a more formal presentation in 1930, as well as in a book in Dutch in 1924.

Windisch's interests as evidenced in published works were wide: the Synoptics; Paul; John; Acts; Revelation (on which he wrote an encyclopedia article in *Die Religion in Geschichte und Gegenwart,* where he also treated "faith" in the New Testament); *II Clement*; religious figures like Lucian of Samosata and Hystaspes (a Persian king, the protector of Zarathustra, reputed author of a second-century A.D. apocalypse); and Germans who wrote on the "Christ-myth" (like the Jewish dramatist, Samuel Lublinski) or who regarded Jesus as a proletarian leader (Max Maurenbrecher). There are certain themes, however, which appear again and again. For example, "The Christian's Transformation from Sinning [*Entsündigung*] according to Paul" was the title of his *Habilitationsschrift* in 1908; the viewpoint is not only incorporated into his book on baptism of that year but also crops up in an essay of 1917 and in his discussion with Bultmann in 1924, and in his view of man with regard to the Sermon on the Mount. Running through a number of his works is an interest in the Spirit and the history-of-religions problems associated with beliefs about the Spirit. Something needs to be noted concerning Windisch's general views in this area, as background to his essays on the Paraclete in John.

Windisch regarded Jesus as a messianic prophet—in terms of the *religionsgeschichtliche* school, as a *theios anēr* or "divine man," a prophetic Spirit-filled teacher, preacher, and wonder-worker. The term *Pneumatiker* is often used; "spiritual person" renders it, but scarcely does justice to what is meant (in the second essay printed here it is given simply as "Pneumatic" or "Pneumatics"). During his brief ministry (which, Windisch, in an article published in 1911, estimated at anywhere from four-and-a-half to six-and-a-half months according to the several Gospel accounts), this Jesus was influenced by the prophetic strain in the Old Testament and Judaism, by Jewish wisdom literature, and the Spirit. Windisch, as a student of the history of religions, places Jesus squarely in an Israelite-Jewish background, yet he also insists that Jesus and his message, even as it is seen in the Sermon on the Mount, are not congenial to orthodox, Talmudic, rabbinical Judaism (cf. *The Meaning of the Sermon on the Mount,* pp. 124-53, especially pp. 144, 148-49, and 152). Windisch makes quite clear his view that Judaism of this sort found even the Jesus of the Sermon on the Mount "intolerable," and that Jesus "destroyed" such Judaism, just as Sadducean and Pharisaic Judaism sent Jesus to the cross precisely because of the views voiced in this Sermon. A book published posthumously in 1935, during the Hitler period, argues that Paul the Jew freed the Gospel further from Judaism.

It is the emphasis on the Spirit, however, which it is important to note here. In an article published in 1928 (in a volume in honor of two Yale professors) Windisch set forth his position that, while none of the references to the Spirit in our gospels are genuine (all of them being redactional and reflecting the church's later experiences), Jesus was actually a *Pneumatiker.* Such a conclusion must be found between the lines, however, since the church suppressed the earliest references—which viewed Jesus thus—in the interests of a later, "higher" Christology. It was, in Windisch's opinion, the Spirit (or Jesus' notion that he had the Spirit) which made him a prophet, armed him with authority, and, one must suppose, saw him through his inner development, from a message such as is found in the parables, the Lord's Prayer, and the Sermon on the Mount (the "Gospel of Galilee") to a deeper message in which he saw soteriological meaning to his death (the "Gospel of Jerusalem"; Mark 10:45, e.g., or the words of institution). The Spirit-filled prophet thus had a strong messianic self-consciousness and could even regard himself as the Son of man.

Paul, according to Windisch, accepted this "Jerusalem Gospel," which he shared with the original apostles; but he developed it, not merely in terms of the Gentile, Hellenistic environment in which he labored, but also out of his own particular experience, out of what Windisch called the "Gospel of Damascus" (referring to Saul of Tarsus' conversion experience on Damascus Road, Acts 9:1-20). The end result, of course, is a gospel which is a far cry from Jesus' "Galilean Gospel," and gives us the sharp contrast to which Liberalism often referred as the "Double Gospel"—that of Jesus of Galilee and that of

Paul. Windisch saw at work here the principles of "continuity" (to a certain extent) and "new creation."

Paul's creativity he explained by the fact that Paul was a *Pneumatiker* just as, in his view, Jesus had been. As a *theios anēr,* or man of the Spirit, Paul thus had an apostolic self-consciousness and a feeling that he was free from sin. (Note Windisch's clash on this latter point with Bultmann's treatment of the Pauline imperatives and also with the traditional formula *simul justus et peccator* ["justified but at the same time a sinner"]; Windisch preferred *simul sanctus et nondum perfectus* ["sanctified but at the same time not yet perfect"].) Hence Paul, too, on the basis of his own somewhat mystical experience with Christ, felt free to reshape the figure of Jesus Christ to meet the needs of the world to which he preached. Erik Beijer, in his analysis of the work of Windisch, suggests that at this point Windisch's way of viewing Paul (and Jesus) was not without influence on Windisch's own otherwise "objective" scholarship: he saw Paul (and John) creating their own pictures of Jesus, not bound by the Synoptic material (which Windisch regarded as permitting a historical picture of Jesus) or by the church's faith, and led only by their personal assumptions and experiences. Possession of "the Spirit" permitted this. Readers limited to English will find in his book on the Sermon on the Mount (pp. 182-85) an example of how Windisch's own "theological exegesis" operated in reading the Spirit into passages in the Sermon.

Since the two essays below deal with the Spirit in the Fourth Gospel, it is necessary to say something about Windisch's views regarding the Johannine literature. He wrote about the Apocalypse several times (he did not believe it was from the same hand as the Gospel or the three epistles), and, in his later years, concentrated on the Gospel of John. A 1923 article holds that the Fourth Gospel is a dramatic work of art standing somewhere between a Synoptic-type gospel and a tragic drama. The Fourth Gospel describes the epiphanies of the divine Christ during his human life. It is not built up from pericopes, as are the Synoptics, but far more reflects the literary hand of an author. The author may stress specific details, but that does not mean he was an eyewitness to the events. In the opinion of Windisch, about A.D. 100, after Mark, Matthew, and Luke were complete, the author of John set out to write a new gospel, which was not to supplement the earlier ones, but to replace them, indeed to drive them out of circulation with their Jewishly-colored and eschatologically-oriented sayings and parables. In this the author of John was doing something akin to what

Marcion and Tatian later sought to do: provide a single gospel-book for the church. In his book published in 1926 on John and the Synoptics, and in several subsequent articles (one posthumous), Windisch set forth these views and examined in detail why John used some Synoptic pericopes and ignored others.

If we ask what sort of man could have taken on the task of creating such a new "absolute" gospel, Windisch answers, as we might expect, that he was a man of strong prophetic, Spirit-filled consciousness, like the *Pneumatiker* who produced the Apocalypse. The "new" sayings of Jesus and the revelation discourses in John are to be explained as arising out of the Spirit-filled Christian community. John's is the Gospel of the Spirit, *the* Gospel, produced under the Spirit, to replace all others. The exact identity of the author is unknown, for he is to be identified neither with John the son of Zebedee nor with the "beloved disciple." His Gospel comes not from the oldest circle of disciples, therefore, but from a later period, and sought to replace older traditions. By now the church had had considerable experience in its mission, in the development of the kerygma, and in experiences of the Spirit. This is how Windisch understood the document in which the verses about the Paraclete occur. The two essays translated below appeared respectively in a 1927 collection of scholarly articles presented to Adolf Jülicher on his seventieth birthday, and a 1933 collection for Rendel Harris' eightieth.

Five "Paraclete sayings" occur in the Gospel of John as it now stands, during the discourse in the Upper Room (John 14:15-17; 14:25-26; 15:26-27; 16:5-11, and 16:12-15). The R.S.V. translates the Greek *paraklētos* by "Counselor."

Needless to say, there has been considerable discussion of these verses and of the chapters in which they stand. Are there two addresses in these chapters which are "doublets"? (For example, 13:31–14:31 and chaps. 15–16, inasmuch as 14:31 closes with the words "Rise, let us go hence," but the discourse goes on unbroken for two more chapters.) Or has the order been disturbed? Do the Paraclete sayings come from a separate source, from which they have been inserted into the discourse(s)? Might this have been a pre-Christian source? While the Paraclete is now identified with the Holy Spirit (14:26), might the term originally have had some other application? (Note that at I John 2:1 Christ, not the Spirit, is called *paraklētos* [R.S.V., "advocate"]. Names for the Holy Spirit might have come from various sources, just as do names and titles for Jesus in the New Testament. "Spirit of truth" [14:17] is now found in documents from Qumran.) Above all, what does John mean by the Paraclete, and how do these references fit in with other references in John to the Spirit and with the general view of the Spirit in the gospels?

Long before Windisch wrote his essays a multiplicity of theories had been advanced. The two-volume English treatment on John by J. H. Bernard in the "International Critical Commentary," published in 1928, gives a picture of some views then prevalent (Vol. 1, pp. xxi-xxii; Vol. 2, pp. 496-98). One of the important German commentaries on John in Windisch's day was that of Walter Bauer (second ed., 1925), which stressed Mandaean backgrounds as likely analogues and explanations for Fourth Gospel material. (The Mandaeans are a semi-Christian group in Mesopotamia rediscovered in the seventeenth century, whose sacred writings contain many expressions akin to those in John. Part of the problem is whether these Mandaeans are pre-Christian or are to be explained from Christian influence.) Friedrich Spitta had previously suggested that the Paraclete referred to Elijah, who, according to Jewish apocalyptic, would return before the messiah and refute the world (Mal. 4:5-6; John 16:8-11). Not long before Windisch took up the problem, Hermann Sasse (now known as a systematician of conservative stamp) argued that the Paraclete was a human personality, one filled with the Spirit, a prophet who would proclaim Christ and creatively continue his revelation—just what the author of the Fourth Gospel did. In that case, the evangelist himself would be the Paraclete, even though the final version of the book identifies the Paraclete with the Spirit.

It is against this background of scholarly discussion in the late twenties that Windisch's essays are to be read. So it is that he argues in the first essay that the Paraclete sayings can be detached from their present setting and can thus be seen to stem from a pre-Christian doctrine of the Paraclete, which John took over, identifying it with the Spirit (a core of references is interpreted by the evangelist and expanded). The Spirit-Paraclete, thus created, would be what sanctions the Perfect Gospel which was meant to replace all others.

Windisch's theorizing about an "angelic advocate" figure in late Judaism as a background for the original Paraclete figure continues to enter into discussion today, especially in light of references to angels at Qumran. (A monograph by Otto Betz on *Der Paraklet* especially explores this area; the English-reader will find a treatment on Qumran angelology in *The Faith of Qumran: Theology of the Dead Sea Scrolls,* by Helmer Ringgren, trans. Emilie T. Sander [Philadelphia: Fortress Press, 1963], pp. 81-93.) The sequence of messengers sent by God (Jesus, then the Paraclete), pointed out by Windisch, is a phenomenon also referred to in a recent article by Raymond Brown, S.S., on "The Paraclete in the Fourth Gospel"; he speaks of it as a "tandem relationship," in which one figure departs and another takes his place (cf. Moses/Joshua; Elijah/Elisha; John the Baptist/Jesus). Windisch's reference to an "economic trinity" is a reminder, like that voiced by Eduard Schweizer in the Kittel *Wörterbuch* article on "Spirit of God," not to regard the Paraclete passages as dealing with "the inner relationships of the Trinity," as later centuries were prone to do. In all these ways what Windisch has to say is far from foreign to later discussions on the Paraclete.

In the second essay Windisch's view again appears that Jesus was a *Pneumatiker,* according to the Synoptic evidence when properly interpreted. He then proceeds to relate this to Jesus and the Spirit in the Fourth Gospel. Here Windisch examines several strands of evidence in addition to the Paraclete sayings—the material about Jesus' baptism (John 1:32ff.) and the idea of an insufflation, Jesus "breathing" the Spirit on his disciples after the resurrection (20:22). He offers what he regards as the genuine Johannine teaching—that Jesus appeared on earth as the one who baptizes with Spirit—and discusses how John's picture fits with the Synoptic evidence.

Obviously much has been written on the topic since Windisch's day. In a survey on *Christianity according to St. John,* published in 1946, W. F. Howard, however, wrote that Windisch had done more than any other single scholar to explore the difficult idea of the Spirit in John. The Qumran material gave obvious impetus to reopening the question, but Otto Betz, in summarizing earlier research at the start of his monograph on the Paraclete (which bears the subtitle " 'The Advocate' in heretical late Judaism, the Gospel of John, and newly discovered Gnostic Writings"), suggests that Windisch's work was the most important literary analysis yet done—though one will also want to agree that literary analysis alone will not solve the meaning of the Paraclete verses.

A recent article by Raymond Brown, in preparation for his "Anchor Bible" treatment of the passages, indicates what some of these problems are, as well as Brown's own views among the current proposals. The exact meaning of the term *paraklētos* remains open. It may have a forensic sense — "advocate" (New English Bible); "counselor" (R.S.V.); or "intercessor" (translators like Moffatt and Goodspeed used "Helper," or even "Friend")—or a non-forensic meaning such as "comforter" (16:6-7) or "encourager." No one English word catches all the nuances in the Paraclete passages. Background likewise remains debated. A Mandaean explanation has lost favor with all save a few scholars. The Jewish background is much more emphasized. Even as Windisch's second essay was appearing, Mowinckel, the Old Testament scholar, published the results of his study into the Jewish source material. Qumran has strengthened that impression; however, no precise Qumran equivalent has turned up. But a syncretistic gnostic background is also a possibility. Brown himself feels the Paraclete is modeled primarily after Jesus.

As for Windisch's opinion that the Paraclete sayings have been interpolated from a pre-Christian source, thereby shifting the view from the the Spirit as a *force* God bestows on men to the Paraclete as a *person* sent to men, Brown calls this a "bad over-simplification," since the Spirit had been regarded as a person prior to John's time (p. 124). Brown's own emphasis is that the Paraclete is "another Jesus," for everything said about him is said about Jesus elsewhere in the Fourth Gospel. The Paraclete answers in particular the problems of (1) the delay of the parousia (he consoles the believer over its delay by bringing Jesus into his life); and (2) the problem of getting along without eyewitnesses (the "beloved disciple" was an incarnation of the Paraclete; now it is the proclamation of disciples under the Paraclete which will continue to make Jesus real). Eduard Schweizer strikes a similar note in his treatment: the Paraclete makes real the church's preaching of Jesus as redeemer; he opens up the truth of Jesus' word and makes possible the life of the Christian community.

The present essays were suggested for inclusion in Facet Books by James W. Cox, Associate Professor of Preaching at the Southern Baptist Theological Seminary, Louisville, Kentucky, and he has served as translator.

In the translation the five Paraclete sayings have been printed out for the convenience of the reader. Those readers who have read Windisch's essays in German will recall that he cited always from the Greek text. In the present edition we have cited from the Revised Standard Version, including the Greek only in those cases where it seemed important to the argument or otherwise helpful.

It should be noted that some of Windisch's terminology does not accord with more recent usage. Thus, he does not distinguish between *Geschichte* and *Historie,* nor does his use of *postexistential* and *postexistentiell* follow the current distinction between "existentialistic" (referring to the philosophical system of Existentialism) and "existential" (for that which belongs to human existence). *Postexistential, post-existentiell,* and *postexistent* derive, in Windisch's essays, from the term *Postexistenz,* meaning "post-earthly existence" (in contrast to *Prae-existenz*). Thus it denotes an outlook in the Gospels which can be described as "post-Easter," and that rendering has been used.

Full bibliographical data on titles referred to in the Introduction will be found at the end of the book in the section "For Further Reading." The Windisch bibliography there is listed chronologically.

JOHN REUMANN

Lutheran Theological Seminary
Philadelphia
July, 1967

Contents

THE FIVE
JOHANNINE PARACLETE SAYINGS

RECENT THEORIES ABOUT THE SAYINGS

RECENTLY, contributions to scholarly discussion of the problem of the Paraclete have come from various quarters.

In an interesting article on "The 'Other' Comforter,"[1] B. W. Bacon showed that two conceptions of the Paraclete run through the entire New Testament: "the friend at court"—the heavenly intercessor (cf. I John 2:1; Rom. 8:31 ff.); and "the friend from court"—the witness sent by God to earth (thus, Mark 13:9 ff.; John 14:15 f.; etc.).

Next, in a stimulating study entitled "Der Paraklet im Johannes-Evangelium,"[2] H. Sasse advanced the hypothesis that we have to distinguish two groups of statements about the Paraclete: those of the older version (John 15, 16), in which the evangelist himself is meant; and those of the later version (John 14), where the Paraclete is identified with the Holy Spirit. In this, he follows F. Spitta to some extent.[3]

In his interesting work *Le quatrième Évangile*[4] H. Delafosse, like Sasse, maintained that the identification of the Paraclete with the Holy Spirit is secondary. Montanus, who called himself the Paraclete but not the incarnation of the Holy Spirit, is still a witness for the non-inter-

[1] B. W. Bacon, "The 'Other' Comforter," *Review and Expositor*, 2 (1917), 274-82.
[2] *Zeitschrift für die neutestamentliche Wissenschaft*, 24 (1925), 260-77.
[3] F. Spitta, *Das Johannes-Evangelium als Quelle der Geschichte Jesu* (Göttingen: Vandenhoeck und Ruprecht, 1910), pp. 316 ff., 358. According to Spitta, the following verses are original: 16:7 f.; 16:12-14; 14:14, 16 (up to "Counselor" [*paraklēton*], omitting "another"); the rest is from the redactor, who also effected the equating of the Paraclete with the Holy Spirit.
[4] Paris, 1925.

polated text.[5] According to Delafosse (pp. 105 ff.), this original document is a Gnostic-Marcionitic work, and the Paraclete—who is still to come—was understood by the author to be Marcion.

Although the last two hypotheses will not find much support, these scholars are proceeding from correct observations. It is the purpose of the following discussion to pursue these investigations further.

My point of departure is the observation that the statements about the Paraclete found in the farewell discourses in the Fourth Gospel constitute five sayings full and complete in themselves: the first, 14:15-17; the second, 14:25-26; the third, 15:26-27; the fourth, 16:5-11; and the fifth, 16:12-15.

The first three sayings indicate most clearly that the statements form small units. They can be removed from the context without leaving a gap, and, in fact, the omission even improves the context.

Apart from the Paraclete references, the entire fourteenth chapter deals with Jesus and the Father, with his going away to the Father and his return. The idea that Jesus comes back to his own *in the Spirit* is nowhere to be found. This is a later combination which rests solely on the fact that the promise of his return, in verses 18 f. and in verse 23 in the modern text, is imbedded between two Paraclete promises.[6] Originally, this insertion had reference to the mystically reinterpreted parousia of Jesus. The authentic primitive Christian understanding of the parousia is still evident in verses 2 f.: Jesus comes again in order to take home his own (cf. I Thess. 4:17). Father and Son send the Spirit; the Son does not descend in the Spirit any more than the Father does. Thus all the Paraclete sayings state clearly that the Spirit comes in the place of Jesus who has gone away and remains in heaven.

The purview of the chapter (apart from the Paraclete sayings) is obviously self-contained. The sending of the Spirit, on the other hand, is an entirely new idea which is not prepared for in what comes before and is not referred to in what follows. The Spirit is a *donum superadditum,* an additional gift received gladly, to be sure, but not anticipated in the first stratum of the chapter and no longer necessary: the disciples have been sufficiently enlightened and comforted with regard to Jesus' departure and absence. What they possess spiritually—and what is here presupposed (expectation of his return, communion with the Father, faith, miraculous power, prayer, obedience, love, the mystical indwelling, peace)—gives them all that they need.

[5] Delafosse lists as interpolations 14:16*b* ("to be with you for ever"); 14:17; 14:26 ("the Holy Spirit"); 15:26 ("the Spirit of truth, who proceeds from the Father"); 16:13 ("the Spirit of truth").

[6] The question of Judas in vs. 22 and the answer given to it in vs. 23 are not related to the Paraclete saying, but to the promise of the return in vss. 18 f.

It is evident that the third saying in 15:26 f. is also an interpolation, for it interrupts the reflections on the world's hatred and on persecution. The saying can be fitted into the context by relating "witness," the subject of the saying, to the defense before the tribunal, and such an interpretation doubtless led to its inclusion in this sequence of thought. However, this interpretation is secondary and much too restricting. Originally, the saying had to do with witnessing in general.

What has been said about the Paraclete sayings in chapter fourteen applies also to those in the fifteenth and sixteenth chapters. The second pattern [*Entwurf*] of the farewell discourses is, again, a complete and self-contained whole without the Paraclete sayings in 15:26 and in 16:5-15. Upon reading in 15:1-17 the allegory of the vine and the entire discourse on the abiding communion of Master and disciples, who would be inclined to think of an intervening advent of the Spirit? In the light of these wonderful attestations of the communion and friendship of the Master, it would be a *paraklētos pareisaktos*.[7] Moreover, the second large section, the section dealing with hatred and persecution (15:18-25; 16:1-4), is carried solely by the terms Father/I/ you/the world. It has a strong dualistic-binitarian orientation. And the last section, 16:16-33, is again unalloyed farewell discourse in the style of chapter fourteen. Verse 22 promises the personal return of Jesus and certifies the hearing and answering of prayer as a bond between the disciples and the Father. It is especially significant that the Spirit is not mentioned in the references to speaking "in figures" and without figures,[8] as when the disciples acknowledge in verses 25-30 that Jesus has already put aside figurative language. Jesus himself has charge of communication with his disciples. Thus the Spirit is not needed at all, either now or in the future.

This confirms our first thesis: *The five Paraclete sayings do not belong in the original text of the farewell discourses.* They are alien entities in the course of both dialogues (chaps. 13-14, 15-16). The latter are intimately related to each other, as is shown in any case by the fact that there is no place in either for a sending of the Spirit. If the latter is allowed into the framework of these discourses, there is a plethora of promises, and an organic structure is possible only if one identifies the sending of the Spirit with the promised return of Jesus. However, this would do violence to the original sense of both promises.

---

[7] [A "Paraclete smuggled in."—TRANS.]

[8] [R.S.V., "plainly," Greek, *en parrēsia* (16:25, 29); R.S.V., "no longer . . . in figures," Greek, *ouketi en paroimiais* (16:25).—TRANS.]

EXEGETICAL ANALYSIS OF THE FIVE SAYINGS

Our five sayings, then, represent something unique and new in contrast to the first stratum of the farewell discourses. They form a complex of tradition that stands in contrast to all the other words of farewell. We must now inquire whether this complex is a unit or whether (with Sasse) we must distinguish two forms of development, and, further, whether the five sayings represent independent logia which have been included in the "farewell discourses" without change. To answer these questions, we must examine more closely the form and content of each independent "saying."

(1) The first saying (14:15-17) does not begin immediately with the promise of the Paraclete. It first lays down a condition: the keeping of Jesus' command as proof of love to him.

> [15]"If you love me, you will keep my commandments. [16]And I will pray the Father, and he will give you another Counselor, to be with you for ever, [17]even the Spirit of truth, whom the world cannot receive, because it neither sees him nor knows him; you know him, for he dwells with you, and will be in you."

The statement of a condition in verse 15 is an abbreviated variation of 15:10.[9] It could also be an independent logion. The concept is new, having been prepared for only by 13:34 f. However, it is easy to insert into the sequence, for it fits well with 14:12 f. (what Jesus will do for the disciples, what they are to do for him), and it is taken up again in verse 21a. Therefore, the statement could have had its place in the original plan [*Entwurf*] of the Gospel. That it nonetheless (also) belongs to the Paraclete saying is shown by the analogous saying in verse 23, an analogy important also in other respects. In this verse, the abiding of Father and Son is likewise made to depend on the expected keeping of the command as proof of love. Thus, verses 15-17 and verse 23 are doublets. It is possible that the introduction to the first Paraclete saying was formed following the pattern of this logion. The variation in content (in the former, the other Paraclete comes in place of Jesus; in the latter, Father and Son come) remains unaffected by this observation.

The body of the Paraclete saying contains statements on the manner of his coming (Jesus prays, and the Father gives), on his function and his nature, and on the ability to perceive him. In the first element there is a good tie with the preceding logion on prayer, except that in the

[9] [15:10 reads: "If you keep my commandments, you will abide in my love, just as I have kept my Father's commandments and abide in his love."—TRANS.]

version in verses 13 f. Jesus himself appears as the fulfiller of the prayer offered in his name. This indicates that the tie is only a loose one and can explain only why the saying was introduced *here.* A second reference back to the preceding logion on prayer seems to be indicated by "another." This defines the role that Jesus plays in the prayer life of the disciples as that of the *primary Paraclete.* Precisely construed, this exists, to be sure, only if Jesus supports God's fulfillment of prayer through his intercession, not if he hears it himself. Therefore, the thought fits better the setting in 16:23 f. At the same time, it is sufficiently motivated by means of the words "and i will pray." Thus, it is no longer absolutely necessary to hold[10] that "another" is a later addition.

In that case, it is unnecessary to think of a "Paraclete in heaven." Jesus, on earth, promises the sending of another Paraclete, who is to remain forever with the disciples. This means that up to this time he himself was their Paraclete—their counselor, companion, and protector —and that his last deed as their Paraclete is to provide a successor.

This also renders superfluous an otherwise quite plausible interpretation, namely, that "another Paraclete" is a reference to I John 2:1, where *paraklētos* has, in any case, the lexicographically more original meaning of "advocate" (in heaven).[11] The Paraclete in heaven is not meant here (in John 14) at all. Only the "Paraclete on earth" is meant (see below).

With the clause "to be with you for ever" our saying proves to be a variant of the great saying of Christ in Matthew 28:20 ("And lo, I am with you always, to the close of the age"). What the Johannine Christ ascribes to the other Paraclete, the Christ of Matthew claims for himself. (Both sayings, incidentally, presuppose a weakening of expectation of the parousia.) However, one may not conclude, therefore, that fundamentally they are the same. John and Matthew represent two entirely different conceptions. Indeed, if Matthew (28:20) were later than John, one could take Matthew 28:20 to be a protest against John 14:16!

The instruction continues with the second name which is given to this new Paraclete; it is, therefore, an interpretation of this name. Here John suggests ideas which call to mind the dualistic views of Paul on the "spiritual man" and the "unspiritual man" in I Corinthians 2:10 ff. Thus the second half of our saying is intended to explain why the Paraclete lends his service to only a small part of mankind and why the

[10] With J. Wellhausen, *Das Evangelium Johannes,* p. 65, and F. Spitta, *Das Johannes-Evangelium,* p. 346. This, incidentally, would presuppose a different word order: *kagō erōtēsō ton patera kai dōsei humin paraklēton.*

[11] On this, compare E. Schwartz, "Aporien im Vierten Evangelium," in *Nachrichten von der Gesellschaft der Wissenschaften in Göttingen,* Vol. 3, p. 187.

world remains a stranger to him. The intimate relation of the Spirit to the disciples is very artfully portrayed with the three prepositions "with you" (*meth' humōn*), "with you" (*par' humin*), "in you" (*en humin*).

John has an analogy to the entire idea in 17:13-19, where the contrast between church and world is carefully considered also. However, the Word is designated as the representative of the Christ who goes to the Father. He leaves this Word behind (as he does peace, according to 14:27), a proof that the promise of the Paraclete is not presupposed in the high-priestly prayer and that it is limited to the five sayings alone.

The nature of the Paraclete-Spirit is not yet clearly stated in this first Paraclete saying. Only this much is certain: the Paraclete-Spirit does not really constitute the power which renders one capable of ethical action, for he is not given until after obedience has taken place. This is best illustrated in Acts 5:32: "the Holy Spirit whom God has given to those who obey him." The Spirit, therefore, must be something different, a power of revelation, an extra-ethical *charisma,* a helper in the specific needs of the church on earth, the power which enables the disciples to persevere by means of what John calls the "truth," and to proclaim this truth and explore it.

(2) The insertion of the second saying, 14:25-26, in the sequence of the farewell discourses is, again, preceded by an introduction (vs. 25):

> [25]"These things I have spoken to you, while I am still with you. [26]But the Counselor, the Holy Spirit, whom the Father will send in my name, he will teach you all things, and bring to your remembrance all that I have said to you."

The mission of the Paraclete is here intimately connected with the teaching work of Jesus which is now about to end. That is already evident in the expression "in my name," which here means something like "on my recommendation" and "in the interest of my work," perhaps even explicitly, "in my stead."

Very significant are the two functions which the Paraclete has to perform as substitute and perpetuator of Jesus on earth. First, he appears as "teacher" (*didaskalos*) and, secondly, as the one who repeats all of the teachings of Jesus. One can, to be sure, regard the two expressions as synonymous or at least link "all that I have said to you" with the first "all." Then the message of the Spirit would be limited entirely to explanation and repetition of the things learned from Jesus.[12]

However, it is more probable that the words "will teach all things"

---

[12] Sasse, "Der Paraklet im Johannesevangelium" (cited above, n. 2), p. 276.

(*didaxei panta*) must be taken independently, and that here, as in the fifth saying, the Spirit is regarded as having another teaching function —namely, to *complete* the teaching of Jesus, as well as to bring it to remembrance. If so, we have to distinguish between a *didachē* of the Paraclete, which is to say, the apostolic kerygma which arose and was consolidated after Easter—the understanding of the words and works of Jesus as developed in the apostolic church (see John 2:22; 12:16)[13]— and a *didachē* of Jesus through the Paraclete, the proclamation of Jesus as the disciples delivered it to the church, thanks to an influencing and strengthening of their powers of recollection by the Spirit. Thus the entire proclamation of the apostles, particularly their share in the transmission of the evangel as inspired, is guaranteed. The church is assured (a) that everything Jesus said is known and preserved, and (b) that the extant tradition of the teaching of Jesus is genuine and trustworthy.

These are the two elements to which Papias, too, calls special attention in the "tradition" which he has heard concerning the Gospel of Mark, when he says, "For he had one purpose only—to leave out nothing that he had heard, and to make no misstatement about it."[14] However, Papias ascribes these two attributes of the evangelist—completeness and trustworthiness—to purely human factors: the relationship of Mark to Peter, his memory ("writing down some things just as he remembered them"),[15] and his conscientiousness ("wrote down carefully . . . all that he remembered").[16]

Here we find one of the few passages in John that could be said to sanction the older gospel tradition.[17] However, within the framework of the Fourth Gospel, with its claim to sufficiency, its autonomy, and its usually thoroughgoing negation of the older writings, it is more accurate to relate the words "He will . . . bring to your remembrance all that I have said to you" to the tradition extant in the Fourth Gospel. Then our saying is stating that the Johannine words of Christ are the repro-

---

[13] This by no means refers exclusively to the ethic of the church then (E. Schwartz, "Aporien im Vierten Evangelium," p. 188).

[14] *henos gar epoiēsato pronoian, tou mēden hōn ēkousen paralipein ē pseusasthai ti en autois* (Eusebius, *Church History,* 3.39.15). Translation from G. A. Williamson (trans. and ed.), Eusebius, *The History of the Church from Christ to Constantine* (Baltimore: Penguin Books, 1965), p. 152.

[15] *houtōs enia grapsas hōs apemnēmoneusen* (Eusebius, *Church History,* 3.39.15). Translation from Williamson, p. 152.

[16] *hosa emnēmoneusen, akribōs egrapsen* (Eusebius, *Church History,* 3.39.15). Translation from Williamson, p. 152.

[17] Cf. A. F. Loisy, *Le quatrième Évangile* (2d ed.; Paris: Nourry, 1921), p. 414.

duction of the apostolic preaching of Jesus,[18] that this record of these words is complete and, having been guided by the Spirit, is absolutely reliable.[19]

(3) The third saying, 15:26-27, is, as we have said, a logion composed altogether independently, which owes its inclusion in this place to a particular, restricting interpretation.

> [26]"But when the Counselor comes, whom I shall send to you from the Father, even the Spirit of truth, who proceeds from the Father, he will bear witness to me; [27]and you also are witnesses, because you have been with me from the beginning."

The introduction, "But when the Counselor . . ." (*hotan elthēi ho paraklētos* . . .) assumes that the figure of the Paraclete is already known.[20] The striking parallelism—

"the Counselor . . . whom I shall send to you from the Father";
"the Spirit of truth, who proceeds from the Father"

—can lead one to suppose that one of the titles is an interpolation. In any case, the second line clarifies the first ("the Counselor" [*paraklētos*] = "the Spirit of truth" [*pneuma tēs alētheias*]) and corrects it in the direction of asserting the sovereignty of the Father.[21] Obviously, the evangelist has an interest in giving exact and correct information about the origin of the Paraclete and the mode of his mission. The evangelist's interest must lie somewhere in the area of a trinitarian faith in revelation: he wishes to teach that the Spirit is one [*solidarisch*] with Jesus and, like him, proceeds from the Father. The Spirit is, then, definitely not an independent revelational entity nor even one arrayed against Jesus. Therefore, whoever confesses the Spirit remains fully

---

[18] Note the "you" (*humas*), and cf. the testimonies in the first person plural in 1:14 and especially in I John 1:5.

[19] See my work, *Johannes und die Synoptiker* (Leipzig: J. C. Hinrichs, 1926), especially pp. 147 f.

[20] Just as 4:24, "when he comes" (*hotan elthēi ekeinos*), refers back to the messiah mentioned previously, and Matt. 25:31, "When the Son of man comes . . ." (*hotan de elthēi ho huios tou anthrōpou* . . .), states that the person of the Son of man and the fact of his coming are known, but that now the finer details of his appearing must be made known.

[21] I hold *ekporeuetai* ("proceeds") to be synonymous with *ekpempetai* ("sent forth") and therefore reject the Catholic interpretation that sees here an eternal emanation of the Spirit from the Father (M. J. Lagrange, *Évangile selon Saint Jean* [Paris: V. Lecoffre, 1925], p. 413).

within the framework of Jesuanic religion. Consequently, the parallelism has didactic, apologetic, and perhaps also polemical intent.[22]

What is said here now about the function of the Paraclete is a generalized repetition of what has been stated already in the second saying: "he will bear witness to me" can comprehend the entire content of the (Johannine) Gospel.

Of all the Paraclete sayings, this third one comes closest to the Synoptic saying concerning the *pneuma*:[23] "And when they bring you to trial and deliver you up, do not be anxious beforehand what you are to say; but say whatever is given you in that hour, for it is not you who speak, but the Holy Spirit" (Mark 13:11; parallels, Matt. 10:19 f., Luke 12:11 f.). As Matthew and Luke have already changed the logion, so John has completely recast it in his own distinctive terminology.[24] It is most remarkable that he has changed the antithesis, "not you, but the Spirit," into a parallel: the Spirit *and* you also! In addition to the witness of the Spirit, the testimony of the disciples, which rests on first-hand experience, is considered.[25] The prohibition is changed into a command just as definite as the prohibition, and the disciples' own testimony is no longer considered inspired. Therefore, the Spirit stands independently beside them with his witness. Here one would be inclined to think of an independent person—a prophet in whom the Spirit is manifested—or of any manifestation of the Spirit at all; in any event, there would come to mind an analogy to the Logos incarnated in Jesus, or a kind of second Messiah (compare the quite analogous statement about the Samaritan Messiah: "when he comes, he will show us all things," John 4:25). If one does not wish to ascribe this view to the evangelist, then one must think either of the wonders and signs closely associated with the Word (cf. Heb. 2:3 f.) or of the actually inspired, ecstatic speaking—glossolalia and prophecy.[26]

Thus, verse 27 has no real intrinsic connection with the Paraclete saying. It could be the evangelist's addition to the saying which had been transmitted or formed independently.

[22] In any event, the designation of the Spirit as the Paraclete has contributed a great deal to the understanding of him as an independent personal being.

[23] But compare further "he will teach you" (*humas didaxei*) in the second saying with Luke 12:12.

[24] On the following cf. H. Sasse, "Der Paraklet im Johannesevangelium" (see above, n. 2), pp. 271 f.

[25] The same coordination is found in Acts 5:32: "And we are witnesses to these things, and so is the Holy Spirit whom God has given to those who obey him."

[26] The latter is probably meant in Acts 5:32.

(4, 5) The fourth and fifth sayings (16:5-11 and 16:12-15) have this in common: both have an introduction (vss. 5-7*a*, 12) in which (with individual differences) the motif of farewell is clearly sounded:

> [5]"But now I am going to him who sent me; yet none of you asks me, 'Where are you going?' [6]But because I have said these things to you, sorrow has filled your hearts. [7]Nevertheless I tell you the truth: it is to your advantage that I go away, for if I do not go away, the Counselor will not come to you; but if I go, I will send him to you. [8]And when he comes, he will convince the world of sin and of righteousness and of judgment: [9]of sin, because they do not believe in me; [10]of righteousness, because I go to the Father, and you will see me no more; [11]of judgment, because the ruler of this world is judged."
>
> [12]"I have yet many things to say to you, but you cannot bear them now. [13]When the Spirit of truth comes, he will guide you into all the truth; for he will not speak on his own authority, but whatever he hears he will speak, and he will declare to you the things that are to come. [14]He will glorify me, for he will take what is mine and declare it to you. [15]All that the Father has is mine; therefore I said that he will take what is mine and declare it to you."

Thus both sayings divide into (a) an introduction concerning the precondition or purpose of the sending of the Spirit and (b) the actual instruction concerning the advent of the Paraclete. The second of these could form the kernel of a primitive logion which, like the third saying (and to some extent the parable of the judgment of the world by the Son of man in Matthew 25:31), was introduced with the familiar expression: "but when the Paraclete comes" (*hotan de elthēi ho paraklētos*).

In the fourth saying the notion that Jesus must leave the stage, since otherwise the Paraclete cannot come, is quite significant. This is a view peculiar to the fourth evangelist, one which sees the death of Jesus as essential for salvation. Beneath all this lies the idea of a chain of witnesses to revelation who must succeed one another in turn: the church must remain constantly under the guidance of a witness. However, while the forerunner of Jesus (according to the evangelist) could still work together with Jesus for a time, the Paraclete can appear only after Jesus has disappeared.

There is here a faint gleam of the succession of two reigns or two ages: the reign of Christ comes to an end so that the reign of the Paraclete can commence.[27] Presupposed is that the coming of the Spirit is a fervent wish of the church.

---

[27] Or does a motif of the heavenly economy underlie this conception: of the two heavenly persons only one can be spared from heaven at any one time?

Verse 8 briefly and succinctly teaches us about the function of the Paraclete. In the third saying this function was designated as "witnessing" (i.e., as apology and, to some extent, still as mission propaganda). Here, in the fourth saying, "convicting" is the function: vis à vis the world the Paraclete fulfills the role of an accuser (Rev. 12:10), a "Satan" (Job 1; Zech. 3:1 ff.).[28] He becomes a preacher of judgment: the three concepts "sin" (*hamartia*), "righteousness" (*dikaiosunē*), and "judgment" (*krisis*) are the basic motifs of prophetic and apostolic preaching of judgment.[29] In that case, however, the somewhat obscure and artificial Christian exegesis in verses 9-11 should be regarded as secondary. That is to say, the kernel of the saying is a logion, verse 8, to which the evangelist has given a meaning relative to his Christ and to the situation of the farewell discourses. The unbelief of the Jews, Jesus' going to the Father, and the judgment upon the lords of this world are three significant themes of the farewell discourses and of the Fourth Gospel in general. They are likewise three important themes of Johannine and primitive-Christian theology. John intends to say, therefore, that the content of his witness to the Christ—both that directed to the believer and that directed to the unbeliever—is an interpretation of the fundamental points of the history of Jesus in the light of the Christian faith, just as the entire apologetic, theology, and polemic of the apostolic community is inspired by the Paraclete and represents his judging and vindicating witness.[30]

(5) What is said in the fifth saying (16:12-15) about the function of the Paraclete leads us back to the second saying. It is explained quite boldly that the Spirit is the fulfiller of the proclamation of Jesus: that is, while Jesus has taught only the little mysteries, the Spirit initiates

[28] [See R.S.V. note on "Satan" at Job 1:6.—TRANS.]

[29] Cf. the New Testament witnesses: John the Baptist; for Jesus perhaps the Sermon on the Mount; for Paul the sayings in I Cor. 6:9f., Gal. 6:7f., and especially Acts 24:25; moreover, the *Didache* (chaps. 1-4, *dikaiosunē;* chap. 5, *hamartia;* chap. 16, *krisis*). Cf. further F. Spitta, *Das Johannes-Evangelium* (see above, n. 3), pp. 319f.

[30] For details cf. the commentaries; for *dikaiosunē* cf. especially W. H. P. Hatch," "The Meaning of John XVI.11," *Harvard Theological Review,* 14 (1921), pp. 103-5. The most artificial interpretation is definitely that of *dikaiosunē*. Is it not likely that the text is corrupted here? That Jesus goes to the Father and the disciples see him no more is the situation of the farewell discourses and the occasion of the promise of the Paraclete, but it is not the demonstration of his *dikaiosunē*. I venture the opinion that the brief passage was inserted here from some other place and has supplanted the original meaning of *dikaiosunē*.

into the great ones; while Jesus was teacher of first principles for the "children" (*nēpioi*), the Spirit can teach the disciples as those who are "mature" (*teleioi*). One can apply this also to the Gospel of John: it is the Gospel inspired by the Paraclete for the mature who have done away with their immaturity (I Cor. 13:11; 3:1 ff.; Heb. 5:11 ff.).

The explanation which now follows (16:13*b*-15) sounds like a correction of the daring concept which seems to place the Spirit above Jesus (an impression one gets also in 14:16, where, however, it is not qualified): the Spirit is not an independent witness who is perhaps even superior to Jesus; he is, rather, wholly dependent on Jesus. To be specific, he is characterized as a prophet or emissary (as is Jesus; cf. 14:10) who is nothing more than the mouth and the organ of his sender. This is the same tendency toward subordination that one finds in certain words spoken by John the Baptist (cf. especially John 1:23; 3:27 f.). The Spirit's witness is given to him by Jesus who, therefore, fulfills his own witness itself through the organ of the Paraclete. That he did not fulfill it on earth lay not so much with him as with the disciples' still immature stage of development (cf. I Cor. 3:1 ff.).

Finally, the content of the Spirit's witness is also given here. It is apocalyptic ("he will declare to you the things that are to come") and glorifies Jesus ("he [the Spirit] will glorify me").[31] That the Spirit announces things to come is a pre-Johannine concept: it finds its realization both in prophetism and apocalyptic. The Apocalypse of John is the most vivid illustration in the New Testament. In the Fourth Gospel "the things that are to come" (*erchomena*) are not very prominent. This motif, too, the fourth evangelist has not invented, although he could have intended it to refer to such prophecies as 14:1 ff. and 15:18–16:4.[32] On the other hand, the second theme is specifically Johannine. The glorification of Jesus is one of the sustaining motifs of the Fourth Gospel. The evangelist means to suggest here that his Gospel, since Jesus is glorified in it, is inspired by the Spirit.[33]

[31] Cf. J. Wellhausen, *Das Evangelium Johannes* (see above, n. 10), p. 72.

[32] In his *Das Johannesevangelium* (Göttingen: Vandenhoeck und Ruprecht, 1900), pp. 151 f. [trans. E. Lummis, *The Gospel according to St. John: An Inquiry into Its Genesis and Historical Value* (Edinburgh: T. & T. Clark, and New York: Scribner's, 1902), p. 163], and *Die Schichten im vierten Evangelium* (Göttingen: Vandenhoeck und Ruprecht, 1911), p. 80, H. H. Wendt considers the expression [*kai ta erchomena anaggelei humin*] an addition. It is, in fact, isolated in the sayings, and if the line is struck out the rhythm is purer. The evangelist, who worked out the interpretation of the Paraclete as referring to the Spirit, could not, however, have added this. It is more likely the product of a glossator who came after the evangelist.

[33] See my work, *Johannes und die Synoptiker* (see above, n. 19), pp. 147 f.

The foregoing analysis has shown us that the five sayings belong together, that they are, to be sure, secondary in the framework of the farewell discourses, but that, formally, the evangelist has nevertheless skillfully worked them in. No attempt is made to adjust the idea underlying these sayings—that the Paraclete represents Jesus who is absent and will remain absent—to the promise of the eschatological or mystical parousia of Jesus, a promise which is essential to the basic conception. It is only to this extent that the inclusion of the five sayings is not carried through. The Pauline idea, that Christ is the Spirit and that he comes in the Spirit, is foreign to John.[34] The concept of the coming of the Spirit is concentrated exclusively in these five sayings which John has incorporated in his Gospel as a supplement and only superficially.[35]

The concept itself did not originate with John himself—he took it over, but added his own interpretation. One can distinguish with a degree of certainty between kernel and interpretation in the third, fifth, and fourth sayings (cf. 14:26; 16:8; 16:13a, on the one hand, and 15:27; 16:9-11; 16:13b-15, on the other hand). Apparently the combination of the Paraclete with the Spirit (*pneuma*) also belongs to the interpretation. The fourth saying is a pure Paraclete saying. In the fifth saying, "the Spirit of truth" (16:13) can be isolated quite easily (note the *ekeinos* in 16:14).[36] Accordingly, in the second and third sayings

[34] This opposes W. Heitmüller, *Das Johannes-Evangelium* ("Die Schriften des Neuen Testaments," 4 vols.; 3d ed. rev.; Göttingen: Vandenhoeck und Ruprecht, 1917), Vol. 4, pp. 151 f.; P. Corssen, "Die Abschiedsreden Jesu im vierten Evangelium," *Zeitschrift für die neutestamentliche Wissenschaft,* 8 (1907), 131 f., 135; H. J. Holtzmann, *Lehrbuch der neutestamentlichen Theologie,* Vol. 2 (2d ed. rev.; Tübingen: J. C. B. Mohr, 1911), pp. 515 f.; P. Feine, *Theologie des Neuen Testaments* (3d ed. rev.; Leipzig: J. C. Hinrichs, 1919), p. 462. The proper distinction is drawn in B. Weiss, *Das Johannes-Evangelium* ("Kritisch-exegetischer Kommentar über das Neue Testament"; Göttingen: Vandenhoeck und Ruprecht, 1902), p. 409.

[35] J. Wellhausen (*Das Evangelium Johannes,* pp. 65 ff.) holds that the Paraclete promises were original and the parousia promises secondary; thus, 14:16 should be joined to 14:1-4. But a parousia is also definitely taught in 14:3 and, in fact, in a setting which makes the sending of a substitute superfluous. However, he is right when he observes (p. 67) that scarcely is the Paraclete introduced before he must disappear again. Yet Wellhausen has not given the explanation for this remarkable situation. Nor does Schwartz give this information. It was already suggested by A. F. Loisy, *Le quatrième Évangile* (see above, n. 17), pp. 414 ff.; however he does not pursue the matter any further. The same is true of A. E. Garvie, *The Beloved Disciple: Studies of the Fourth Gospel* (London: Hodder and Stoughton, 1922), p. 152, who says that the four passages on the Spirit could have belonged originally in another context and then have been transplanted here.

[36] See H. Sasse, "Der Paraklet im Johannesevangelium" (see above, n. 2), p. 275; F. Spitta, *Das Johannes-Evangelium,* pp. 314 ff.

one could also explain the somewhat longer phrasing with respect to the "Spirit" as secondary. The rhythm which is peculiar to both sayings does not directly favor such a view; however, the rhythm of the original sayings could have been distorted somewhat by the interpolation. In the first saying, the statement about the Spirit is not added in apposition to the subject, but linked with the word about the Paraclete as the second half of the saying; specifically, it is an interpretation of the still unfamiliar title of the Paraclete. And all further statements in the canonical text about the Paraclete, who is the Spirit, refer back to this interpretation (14:17). Organically, the sayings belong together. Taking it all in all, this hypothesis is highly plausible: underlying the five sayings is a "Teaching on the Paraclete" written in short logia; this "Teaching" the evangelist took over and interpreted (1) by identifying the Paraclete with the Spirit known to the church and (2) by focusing his witness entirely on the person of the Christ who will depart and be absent. That we can no longer reconstruct the transmitted logia down to their wording does not invalidate our hypothesis.[37]

If we distinguish, then, between transmitted sayings and Johannine recension, we nonetheless conceive of all five sayings—both in what is probably their original form and in their recension—as a unit. Sasse's hypothesis, that the passages in the second discourse (chap. 15 f.) have a different and more primitive character than those in the first discourse has, in our opinion, not proved tenable. In particular, I can perceive no profound distinction between the second saying and the fifth.[38]

THE "PARACLETE" FIGURE

Finally, we have yet to ask the important question of the meaning and origin of the Paraclete figure in our sayings.[39]

According to John, the Paraclete has a double function: for the disciples he will be teacher, the one who brings to mind the teaching of Jesus, continues and finishes his work of revelation, heralds the future and reveals the glory of Jesus, and, finally, is their constant companion

[37] I would isolate the interpolations somewhat as does Delafosse (*Le quatrième Évangile;* see above, n. 4), but I ascribe them in the main to the evangelist and not to the later redactor.

[38] Cf. H. Sasse, "Der Paraklet im Johannesevangelium," pp. 275 f.

[39] On this see most recently, H. Sasse, *ibid.,* pp. 274 ff., 276 f.; further, F. Spitta, *Das Johannes-Evangelium,* pp. 315, 319 f.; W. Bauer, *Das Johannesevangelium* (2d ed.; Tübingen: J. C. B. Mohr, 1925), pp. 177, 181, 191 ff.; J. Wellhausen, *Das Evangelium Johannes,* p. 66; A. Jülicher, "Paraclete," *Encyclopaedia Biblica,* ed. T. K. Cheyne and J. S. Black (New York: Macmillan, 1902), Vol. 3, cols. 3567 ff.

and protector.[40] For the world, he will serve as witness in Jesus' cause and as prophetic attorney who reveals the truth about Jesus and about his adversary, the prince of this world, and who convicts the unbelieving of their errors.[41] Is this entire series of functions to be derived from the concept of the Paraclete, or has the interpretation connecting Paraclete and Spirit added some new titles?

The first question is to what extent these functions can be derived from the title "Paraclete." Proof is no longer needed that the Paraclete (*peraqlêt*) in its original meaning is the intercessor who opposes the accuser (Greek, *katēgoros*; rabbinic loan word, *qāṭêgôr*) before the (human and divine) tribunal and gains the acquittal of the accused.[42] Thus already in Jewish speculation an angel is placed in opposition to Satan; at the angel's word, God shows compassion and justice to mankind.[43] The Paraclete in this sense functions in heaven before the divine judgment seat.

The actual Christian bearer of this role of the Paraclete is Jesus Christ himself. However, he is so named explicitly only in I John 2:1. Without the name *paraklētos* being used, Jesus (the Son of man)

[40] So in the second, fifth, and first sayings.

[41] So in the third and fourth sayings.

[42] See now especially H. L. Strack and P. Billerbeck, *Kommentar zum Neuen Testament*, Vol. 2 (Munich: C. H. Beck, 1924), pp. 560 ff.; H. Cremer and J. Kogel (eds.), *Wörterbuch der neutestamentlichen Gräzität* (Gotha: F. A. Perthes, 1915), pp. 571 ff., English edition, *Biblico-Theological Lexicon of New Testament Greek*, trans. W. Urwick (Edinburgh: T. & T. Clark, 1895 [1954]), pp. 337 ff. Further T. von Zahn, *Das Evangelium des Johannes* (Leipzig: A. Deichert, 1908), pp. 554-58, on John 14:16.

[43] The primary reference is Job 33:23. The obscure word *mēlîs* used there is rendered in the Targum as *peraqlêt;* the synonym *senêgôr* (Greek, *sunēgoros*) is used by the rabbis more frequently. The Greek *Testaments of the Twelve Patriarchs* translates it with *mesitēs* ["mediator"] in the Testimony of Dan. 6:2 (the activity of the *mesitēs* is rendered by *paraiteisthai*, "to intercede"). See Billerbeck, *loc. cit.* In Philo, *De vita Mosis* 2.134 (155), *paraklētos* is the Son of God, i.e., the cosmos whom the high priest takes with him as his paraclete when he approaches God (see J. Grill, *Untersuchen über die Entstehung des vierten Evangeliums* [Tübingen: J. C. B. Mohr, 1902-1923], Vol. 1, pp. 133 ff.; Vol. 2, pp. 331 ff.); *De specialibus legibus* 1.237 (247) designates as paraclete—whom one calls in when one prays in the Temple for forgiveness of sins—*ho kata psuchēn elegchos*, i.e., the conscience (cf. *elegxei* in John 16:8); cf. also the three *paraklētoi* in *De praemiss et poenis* (= *De execrationibus*) 166 (436). Philo still uses the word *paraitētes* as a synonym; see *De mutatione nominum* 129 (598) and *De specialibus legibus* 2.25 (274). According to Schwartz, "Aporien im Vierten Evangelium" (see above, n. 13), pp. 186 f., all of this has only the word in common with the Paraclete of Christians. We shall see how far this judgment is justified; it is, in any case, not true of I John 2:1. See further, F. Büchsel, *Der Geist Gottes im Neuen Testament* (Gütersloh: C. Bertelsmann, 1926), pp. 497 ff.

appears as intercessor in the Synoptic logion Matthew 10:32 (= Luke 12:8) and as *katēgoros* at the same time, to be sure, in the antithesis belonging to this logion, Matthew 10:33, Luke 12:9 (= Mark 8:38), Luke 9:26 (cf. also the parable in Luke 13:6-9). The idea of intercessor appears even more clearly in Paul, in Romans 8:34 (similarly also in Heb. 2:17 f.; 4:14-16; 9:24).

Accordingly, the distinguishing characteristic of the Johannine Paraclete sayings is that another person appears as Paraclete, and Jesus is in this respect plainly overshadowed. To be sure, this person has only the name Paraclete in common with him. The Paraclete in John is in no way portrayed as intercessor on earth for the disciples. The actual idea of an intercessor who blunts accusation and makes a defense shines through only in the third and fourth sayings insofar as the witness and reproof offered by the Paraclete aim at the glorification of Jesus, his vindication. Therefore, he is not so much "the advocate of the disciples in their conflict with the world"[44] as he is the advocate of Jesus, Jesus' defender, or the representative of the absent Jesus before the tribunal of the world.[45] However, this element is not stressed; rather, the reverse side of the exponent's role is emphasized— accusation, conviction, and cogent testimony against the enemy. The intercessor is, therefore, much more the accuser. That is a dialectic species of the concept of intercessor; however, the point of departure is still clearly perceptible here.[46]

Therefore, the Paraclete is to be taken here in a more general sense as witness: witness before the world, witness for Jesus (indirectly also for the disciples), witness against the world (Mal. 3:5). Another development of the concept is found in the first saying, where the Paraclete is described as constant companion and, therefore, as helper and aide [*Beistand*], as patron and protector. For this terminology one can refer perhaps to *Didache* 5:2, *plousiōn paraklētoi* ["advocates of the rich"]. The special functions of *paraiteisthai* ["to intercede"] and *entugchanein* ["to intercede"] can naturally be included here.

---

[44] So A. Schlatter, *Die Geschichte des Christus* (Stuttgart: Calwer, 1920), p. 460.

[45] Cf. Bion as quoted in Diogenes Laertius, 4.50: *to hikanon soi poiēsō, phēsin, ean paraklētous pempsēis, kai autos mē elthēis* [" 'I will satisfy your demand,' he said, 'if you will send advocates and not come yourself' "]; here the Paraclete is exponent and representative of the (absent) suppliant. Is the nuance of "representative" perhaps also to be understood as involved in the Johannine Paraclete sayings?

[46] That *elegchein* ["convince," "convict"] is a function of the Paraclete is shown by the passage from Philo cited above (*De specialibus legibus* 1.237 (247).

16

The Paraclete of the second and fifth sayings, on the other hand, deviates widely from his original function. He does not deal with the salvation and the protection of individuals, but with the main thing, the revelation of the teaching of Jesus: his task is teaching, maintaining, and completing the historical revelation in Jesus. He has a definite message to deliver. He is bearer of a tradition already extant and bearer of a new revelation supplementing and completing it. He is *didaskalos* and *prophētēs,* teacher of tradition and prophet in one and the same person (cf. the scribe referred to in Matt. 13:52).

Now this office, too, can surely be connected with the work of the "witness." The witness of the Paraclete in the church—the vindication of Jesus and the refutation of enemies—grows, then, more and more into a comprehensive reproduction of the teaching of the departed one and, finally, into an inspired supplement to this teaching. Yet this function can still be derived directly from the concept of the Paraclete, namely, from the meaning "counselor" [*Ratgeber*], which certainly appears on occasion for *paraklētos.*[47] The situation of the disciples might be compared with that of a young king who, after his father's death, has standing at his side as counselor an official attendant of the late king (cf. II Kings 12:6ff). This counselor "recalls" the words and deeds of the father. He makes up what is lacking in the father's instruction and completes it, with the father being regarded as the actual teacher (Matt. 11:27a).[48]

Thus the meaning of the Paraclete in our sayings is unfolded in three directions: (1) witness that vindicates and judges; (2) helper and aide; (3) counselor and teacher. The picture of the interceding angel or interceding Christ has receded entirely. What we have is more the image of a prophet who, after the departure of the chief prophet, substitutes for him and now stands at the side of the orphaned church as witness, helper, counselor, and teacher. In this sense Joshua, as Moses' successor, was the "paraclete" of the nation Israel (cf. Deut.

[47] So Philo, *De opificio mundi* 23 (5): *oudeni de paraklētōi—tis gar ēn heteros; — monōi de autōi chrēsamenos ho theos egnō dein euergetein atamieutois kai plousiais charisi tēn . . . phusin . . .* ["Now God, employing no counselor—for who was there besides Him?—but acting solely on his own, perceived that it was necessary to endow nature with rich and unrestricted gifts"]. The citation may be a reminiscence of Isa. 40:13 (= Rom. 11:34); then *paraklētos* = *sumboulos,* i.e., instructor, adviser (A. Jülicher [see above, n. 39]). F. Büchsel, *Der Geist Gottes im Neuen Testament,* pp. 498f., thinks otherwise.

[48] Perhaps this expansion of the *paraklētos* concept belongs with the usage of *parakalein,* which in Christian terminology comprehends all forms of admonition, encouragement, and instruction.

17

18:15 = Acts 7:37); Elisha, as Elijah's successor, was the paraclete (cf. II Kings 2:1 ff.); or (if we ignore the concept of succession) Nathan was the paraclete of David. In brief, in John the figure of a prophet witnessing, giving counsel, teaching, and disclosing the future is really fused with the Paraclete.

Spitta has advanced the interesting hypothesis[49] that the original referrent of *paraklētos* might have been the returning prophet Elijah. He thinks it likely for these reasons: Elijah, too, appears occasionally in the role of an intercessor for the Israelites; the Paraclete of John, too, is also designated a mighty preacher of repentance; finally, the explanation of the Torah and the solution of all unsolved problems of the Law are awaited from Elijah. Admittedly, the Elijah of biblical-Jewish apocalyptic is only the forerunner of Yahweh or of the Messiah, not the successor and fulfiller of the revelation of the Messiah. Nevertheless, we can say that the Paraclete of John has significant points of similarity to Elijah *redidivus*.

The Paraclete may be compared also with the Baptist, this Elijah of the New Testament. He is a witness for Jesus, teaches the disciples about him, and, at least in the Synoptics, is also a preacher of judgment and repentance. The Paraclete, therefore, is in every respect a counterpart to John. In the Fourth Gospel, Jesus has a forerunner and a successor. Both are to bear witness to him. To put it another way: according to John, the gospel rests on the continuity of three witnesses sent from God.[50]

I should like to refer to still another figure from early Christian literature who is related to the Paraclete: the shepherd in the *Shepherd* of Hermas. As John promises the sending of the Paraclete, so Hermas depicts the history of a quite similar mission. The "shepherd" is sent from the most venerable angel (Michael-Christ) to live with Hermas from now until the end (*Visions* 5:2; cf. John 14:16). He has to keep watch over repentance (*Similitudes* 10:1, 3); so his task, too, is to convince "of sin and of righteousness and of judgment" [John 16:8], for he is the punishing shepherd (*ho poimēn ho timōrētēs, Similitudes* 7:1). He gives precepts and parables and so, as interpreter, leads into all truth, thus playing the role of prophetic teacher. In particular, in several of his parables (*Similitudes* 5) he bears witness also to the "Son" as well as to the impotence of the devil (*Mandates* 12:6). In

---

[49] *Das Johannes-Evangelium* (see above, n. 3), pp. 318f.
[50] Instinctively one calls to mind the threefold witness of water, blood, and Spirit (= the Baptist, Jesus, the Paraclete), I John 5:6f. However, this cannot be meant here, for the water *and* blood are connected with the appearing of Jesus.

the parable of the building of the tower, he intervenes actively and cooperates in the building of the church, following the instruction of the Lord in order to prepare for his return (*Similitudes* 9:5 ff.). In line with this, the care of the church on earth is entrusted to him during the Lord's absence. Therefore, he is angel of repentance, prophet of judgment, instructor and advisor, teacher and interpreter, guardian angel and shepherd of souls, church builder and church leader—all in one person.[51] Thus he unites in himself various characteristics of the Paraclete as portrayed by John; even traces of the entire special function of the intercessor (and accuser) before God are found occasionally (*Similitudes* 10:1, 2 ff.).[52] "Paraclete" would be an appropriate title for the angel of repentance too.

However, this does not mean that the Johannine Paraclete goes back to the original figure of the "shepherd," nor does it mean that Hermas has portrayed the fulfillment of the Johannine prediction of the Paraclete or that he was influenced in his sketch of the shepherd by the Johannine Paraclete. The latter is quite improbable.[53] Naturally, the former is not impossible. It is more correct simply to record the fact that there are points of contact between the "shepherd" himself and the Paraclete and that the Paraclete has a colleague—indeed, almost a double—in the angel of repentance and shepherd of Hermas as well as in the interceding angel, in Elijah, and in the Baptist.[54]

He has a double also in the Messiah; or better, he also has about him something of the double of the Christ or of Jesus Christ. Like Jesus, he is an "emissary." Like him, he witnesses and teaches. He is his successor (14:16), and his witness, like the witness of Jesus, deals with the Son of God. Like Jesus, he is, on the one hand, Paraclete and intercessor, and on the other hand, preacher of judgment and accuser.[55]

---

[51] See the excursus by M. Dibelius in *Der Hirt des Hermas* ("Handbuch zum Neuen Testament," Supplementary Vol. 4; Tübingen: J. C. B. Mohr, 1923), pp. 494 ff., which, however, as indicated above, still is not exhaustive.

[52] Cf. especially *Similitudes* 10.2.2 ff.: *bene enim de te hic apud me existimavit,* and *ut . . . et hic apud me de his bene interpretetur et ego apud dominum* ["for he has given me a favorable report of you," and "so that . . . he may recommend them to me, and I to the Lord"].

[53] See T. von Zahn, *Der Hirt des Hermas untersucht* (Gotha: F. A. Perthes, 1868), pp. 465 ff.; C. Taylor, *The Witness of Hermas to the Four Gospels* (London: C. J. Clay, 1892). To be sure, in *Mandates* 3.4 Hermas uses the concept of the "Spirit of truth," *pneuma tēs alētheias,* but the context has nothing to do with the Paraclete sayings. Cf. further *Mandates* 11.5 (*aph' heautou lalei panta*) with John 16:13; here again the view is totally different.

[54] Even if Jesus, according to John 14:16 (see above, p. 5), has been the Paraclete of the disciples on earth, that is very comparable to the work of the shepherd of Hermas.

[55] On the *elegchein* of the Messiah compare *Psalms of Solomon* 17.27.

Like the Messiah of the Samaritan woman (John 4:25), he explains still unanswered questions. Like the glorified Christ (Matt. 28:20), he is with the disciples eternally. In a Jewish writing, the paraclete (as Elijah *redidivus,* who prepares the way for the parousia of Yahweh himself) would become a substitute figure for the Messiah. In the Gospel of John, his sending had to be subordinated to that of the Christ. Only in the fifth saying is there a sudden glimpse of a thought which ascribes a certain superiority to him; however, the necessary restriction is immediately supplied.

This role of the Paraclete as a "double" becomes evident directly from John, not only from the expression about the "other Paraclete" in 14:16, but also from the comparison with the intercessory function of Jesus in heaven in 16:26 as well as from I John 2:1 (Jesus is the Paraclete of the church with the Father). According to John (the Gospel and the first epistle), the church has two intercessors, one in heaven and one on earth—the one, the friend at court who stays at the court and intercedes there for his protégé, and the other the friend from court who is sent by the court and appears in the world as mediator, admonitor, teacher, and ambassador. It is remarkable to discover (with Bacon) that the Synoptics, as well as Paul, are aware of a similar duality of intercessors: in Q the intercessor-Son of man at the divine court of justice (see above) and the Spirit as intercessor on earth (cf. below); in Paul, the Christ at the right hand of God and the Spirit who intercedes for us in our prayers (Rom. 8:34; 8:26 f.).[56] The application of the concept varies, and the link between both functions is loose; however, analogies do exist.

The fourth evangelist has not left his reader in doubt as to the identity of the (other) Paraclete: it is the Holy Spirit. No matter what one may think about the integrity of the Paraclete sayings, it is certain (and at this point I am in agreement with Delafosse and Sasse) that the Spirit and the Paraclete are originally two very different figures. The Spirit is, according to his nature, power, an incomprehensible being that suddenly enters into man and imparts to him impulses and insights which lift him above his human existence. The Paraclete is a concrete heavenly person, a kind of angel, and when he appears on earth, it is as an emissary from God, as an angel in human form or as a prophet, as a teacher sent from God (3:2) and subordinated to the incarnate Logos but yet comparable to him (thus especially in the

---

[56] Both times Paul uses the technical word *entugchanei* ("intercedes"). The Paraclete, whom, according to Philo, the high priest takes with him (see above, n. 43), is the "friend at court."

fourth, fifth, and second sayings). We are unable to say more about the original pre-Johannine meaning of the term.

Sasse's hypothesis (pp. 274 ff.), that in the oldest sketch of the farewell discourse (see 15:16) the evangelist was referring to himself when he mentioned the Paraclete and to his own Gospel when he mentioned the Paraclete's message, and that only later did someone make the connection between the Paraclete and the Spirit (thus in John 14) and then interpolate it into the older text (16:13)—this hypothesis, as we saw, proceeds, to be sure, from correct observations. One can, indeed, read the fourth and fifth sayings as referring to the fourth evangelist and his message, but this cannot be the only reference intended. The three points mentioned in 16:9-11 do not emerge in John with equal weight and clarity, least of all the third. Further, the announcement of things to come (16:13) is not of essential moment in John. Sasse extricates himself by saying that the mention of things to come points to the Apocalypse of John, "which must surely stand in some kind of relation to the Gospel" (p. 274). Whoever sees this "relation" (one asserted also in Lohmeyer's fine commentary) as a very loose one will not be satisfied by this explanation.[57] We therefore reject this hypothesis. The evangelist himself has doubtless already worked out the interpretation of the Paraclete as referring to the Spirit. If so, then the wording of the fourth and fifth sayings indicates only that he regards his Gospel, too, as a proclamation of the Paraclete-Spirit and thought of himself as a bearer of the message of the Paraclete. He suggests here something of the origin and the tendency of his testimony deposited in his Gospel, of the authority which one who was not an apostle had received in order to write a—rather *the*—Gospel which would accomplish the great reckoning with unbelievers and the glorification of Jesus in his earthly manifestation.[58]

Naturally, I must reject also the audacious linking of the Paraclete with Marcion.[59] The impossibility of deriving the Fourth Gospel from Marcionite circles is already an argument against it.[60] It is doubtless true, as Delafosse has rightly observed, that the Paraclete sayings (dis-

[57] In my opinion, the relationship to the Apocalypse would be possible only if (with Wendt) we ascribe the line to a glossator, from which one could assume that he knew the Apocalypse and lived altogether in apocalyptic. [For the reference to "Lohmeyer's commentary," see E. Lohmeyer, *Die Offenbarung des Johannes* ("Handbuch zum Neuen Testament," 16; Tübingen: J. C. B. Mohr, 1926), pp. 198-99. Lohmeyer believed that the Fourth Gospel and Revelation were by the same author, though not the traditional John.—EDITOR.]

[58] See my book *Johannes und die Synoptiker* (see above, n. 19), pp. 148 ff.

[59] H. Delafosse, *Le quatrième Évangile* (see above, n. 4).

[60] Against this derivation see my *Johannes und die Synoptiker,* pp. 172 ff.

regarding their reference to the Holy Spirit) are so concretely conceived that Marcionites could have found in them their great interpreter Marcion, and Montanists, the prophet Montanus. The creator of the sayings certainly had no definite person in mind as yet; he has only clothed in words the general phenomenon.

The interpretation of the Paraclete as referring to the Spirit, which has been brought into the sayings by the evangelist, has, as already said, its analogy both in the Synoptic logia tradition and in Paul. If, according to Mark 13:11 and parallel passages, the Spirit is to speak before the tribunal for the disciples, this can be regarded as witness of the "intercessor." Of the sayings, the third comes closest to this Synoptic logion. The second saying, "he will teach you all things" (*ekeinos humas didaxei panta*), is particularly reminiscent of the Lucan version (Luke 12:12, "for the Holy Spirit will teach you in that very hour what you ought to say"; *to gar hagion pneuma didaxei humas en autēi tēi hōrai ha dei eipein*). The fifth saying more nearly gives the content of the witness intended in the logion. The Paraclete sayings are variants of the Synoptic logion, and John is certainly inspired by it also.

Through his own experience Paul also knows the Spirit as intercessor (Rom. 8:26 f.). However, this special function in our prayer life is unknown to John (John knows only the name of Jesus as help for our prayer). Perhaps Paul has more clearly perceived the real meaning of the nature of the intercessor than John. Another distinction is that in Paul the Spirit, quite like the angel-paraclete of the Jews, fulfills his office as intercessor *before God,* while John has in mind primarily the appearing of the witness in the world. That John may be influenced by Paul in the Paraclete sayings[61] cannot be proved.[62]

The equating of the Paraclete with the Spirit seems quite obvious to John. Not only does the office of intercessor belong to the Spirit, but also the office of witness and the office of teacher and counselor. If the Paraclete is designated in our writing as a prophet, then it is as a prophet who is the bearer of the Spirit. In passages such as Isaiah 11:2, Haggai 2:5, and Psalm 143:10, the Spirit[63] is plainly described

[61] So, for example, C. Clemen, *Die Entstehung des Johannesevangeliums* (Halle: M. Niemeyer, 1912), p. 256.

[62] One must not put so high an estimate on the Pauline influence in John generally, as often happens, or did happen.

[63] Cf. P. Volz, *Der Geist Gottes* (Tübingen: J. C. B. Mohr, 1910). According to Billerbeck (see above, n. 42), Vol. 2, p. 562, the Holy Spirit is once depicted in the Talmud (*Leviticus Rabbah* 6) as "protector." The "Spirit of truth" (*pneuma tēs alētheias*) as judging power (John 16:8 ff.) appears also in the Testament of Judah 20.5.

as a paraclete. One trait in the Johannine Paraclete sayings is probably determined exclusively by the tradition of the Spirit, namely, his imperceptibility, 14:17; this motif also can only have been brought in with the interpretation relating the Paraclete to the Spirit. The explicit identification of the Paraclete with the Spirit is not to be considered original. However, according to his origin the Paraclete is a person already related to the Spirit. In the full development of his nature, he is closer to the Spirit than to the angel of intercession.

The view that the Spirit-Paraclete will appear after the departure of Jesus, as a new, second or third emissary from heaven, is in John expressed exclusively in the Paraclete sayings. Only an allusion, at best, is found in the exegesis which John 7:39 gives of the logion in 7:37 f.; however, what is meant here—the performance of spiritual deeds—is prominent in none of the sayings. The account of the insufflation of the Spirit by the risen Christ (20:22 f.) stands in utter contrast to the promises concerning the Paraclete. The Paraclete is sent from heaven by the Father in cooperation with Jesus; there is no mention in the sayings of the authority to forgive sins. Nor do the sayings betray awareness of the Spirit's being tied to the sacrament of baptism (3:5 ["born of water and the Spirit"]); and the relationship between the Spirit and Jesus which is presupposed in the tradition about Jesus' baptism (1:33 ["He on whom you see the Spirit descend and remain, this is he who baptizes with the Holy Spirit"]) cannot be brought into harmony with the sayings. In this passage, according to an ancient adoptionist view, the Spirit is the equipment which Jesus receives for his earthly ministry, and the "baptizing with the Spirit" is a function which the historical Jesus already exercises; the Spirit, therefore, has already come with Jesus (cf. also 3:34).[64]

In the Johannine epistle, too, the characteristic Paraclete motifs are absent. That the community has the Spirit is nowhere depicted as the fulfillment of the promise of Jesus. The conceptions of the anointing, in I John 2:20, 27, and of the Spirit as the third witness together with water and blood, in 5:6-8, have nothing to do with the idea of the Paraclete.[65] Only the witness in itself and the designation of its nature as "truth" (*alētheia*), and perhaps also the confession in I John 4:2, connect the Spirit with the Paraclete of the Gospel. That God has given us of his Spirit (I John 4:13; 3:24) is at best a quite vague allusion to the Paraclete sayings. That Jesus is designated in I John 2:1 as our Paraclete with the Father, as if we had no other, is like-

[64] See on this point H. J. Holtzmann, *Lehrbuch der neutestamentlichen Theologie* (see above, n. 34), Vol. 2, pp. 508 ff.
[65] Cf. above, n. 50.

wise significant.[66] In my opinion, these facts are still no proof that the epistle came from an author other than the evangelist;[67] they, too, indicate the singular nature of the "Paraclete Sayings," singular even for John.

The idea of the Paraclete sayings is distinguished from all these conceptions especially by "the astounding doctrine"[68] that the appearing of the Spirit is presented as a sending of a new heavenly messenger (who, after the disappearance of Jesus, is sent with the cooperation of the Lord abiding in heaven). "Are you he who is to come, or shall we look for another?" (*ē allon prosdokōmen*), John the Baptist had his disciples ask Jesus (Luke 7:19; Matt. 11:2). According to the evangelist John, Jesus actually promised at his departure that he would pray to the Father for the coming of "another counselor" (*allos paraklētos*; 14:16). The decisive factor, therefore, is the expectation and sending of a new helper from heaven who takes over the function of the earlier emissary. Such consecutive sendings are already known from the Israelite-Jewish history of the prophets. They are summarized in the wisdom saying in Matthew 23:34 (= Luke 11:49) and in the (post-Easter) parable of the vineyard where the sending of the son climaxes the embassies. The evangelist John has assiduously ignored the sending of the prophets,[69] has recognized only that of the Baptist as a preparatory sending (admittedly with the stipulation that it was consumed wholly in witness for his Christ), and now—this is of greatest importance—in view of the need and experience of the day provided a further sending which follows upon the sending of the Son, since the latter had run its course. In doing so, the evangelist takes the greatest pains to stifle any idea that this last sending might be—as it actually should be—the highest and most eminent.[70]

An unmistakable peculiarity of our Paraclete sayings, then, is still their trinitarian character. It is worked out most forcefully in the first and in the third sayings. The idea of the Trinity is worked out in these two ways: the Father has two Paracletes whom he sends to

[66] It was pointed out above that John 14:16, with "another Counselor" (*allon paraklēton*), is in no way connected with I John 2:1.

[67] On this point, see Holtzmann, *Lehrbuch der neutestamentlichen Theologie*, Vol. 2, pp. 517 f.

[68] So Oswald Spengler, *Der Untergang des Abendlandes* (Munich: Beck, 1922-23), Vol. 2, p. 277; trans. C. F. Atkinson, *The Decline of the West: Perspectives of World History* (New York: Knopf, 1926-28), Vol. 2, p. 227.

[69] Cf. the gnostic invective in 10:8, and my book *Johannes und die Synoptiker*, pp. 172 ff.

[70] See above, pp. 7 f. 11 f. Paul also has the paralleling of the sending of the Spirit with that of the Son. It is most clearly expressed in Gal. 4:4-6 (cf. the twice repeated *exapesteilen* ["sent forth"]).

mankind, one after the other [14:15-17]; or, the Spirit is sent by two divine persons, Father and Son [15:26-27]; the former reflects the historical aspect, the latter, the post-Easter aspect. That the Spirit or "intercessor" may be the integrating member of a Trinity, one can hardly say. The intercessor given is rather the son, that is, the king's son, the crown prince.[71] The Trinity originates here rather through addition of a second Paraclete, and this is occasioned by the special circumstances of the Christian history of revelation [*Geschichtsoffenbarung*]. Jesus, "the son," returns to heaven or is in heaven and cannot immediately come back to earth. However, since the congregation needs a helper on earth, a second representative must be sent to it. The Johannine Trinity, therefore, is essentially economically oriented,[72] and its presupposition—this is important—is the receding of faith in the parousia and the lack of the experience of a mystical indwelling of Christ himself. The Spirit must come because Christ remains in heaven and does not come to his own, even in an invisible, mystic manner. That the sending of the Spirit may be his mystical parousia is only later speculation, but the fourth evangelist indeed plays a role in its development. By interposing the promise of the Paraclete between the promises of the parousia (14:1 ff.; 14:18 ff.; 16:16 ff.)—both are originally mutually exclusive and cancel each other out—he suggested the view that the parousia takes place in the sending of the Spirit.[73]

One final word on the origin of the Johannine Paraclete idea. If one proceeds from the use of the word *paraklētos,* then the closest analogy is the interceding angel of Judaism[74] and the *kosmos paraklētos* of Philo.[75] The difference lies only in the fact that the Johannine Paraclete-Spirit discharges his office not in heaven, but on earth (i.e., as "the friend from court"). This turns out to be true of Philo's Logos, who comes precisely into our earthly existence and stands by men and helps (*arēgei kai boēthei*) those who are sympathetic to virtue and

[71] See H. Zimmern, *Vater, Sohn und Fürsprecher in der babylonischen Gottesvorstellung* (Leipzig: J. C. Hinrichs, 1896), pp. 9 f.

[72] [In the "economic" view of the Trinity the divine monarchy is regarded as unfolding in three steps or stages in the course of *Heilsgeschichte* and the revelation of God; the triad or Trinity thus involved is not thought of in terms of "essence" or "substance," but functionally. Cf. G. L. Prestige, *God in Patristic Thought* (London: SPCK, 1952; reprint, 1964) pp. 57-67, 98-106.— EDITOR.]

[73] See further on the Trinity in my commentary *Der zweite Korintherbrief* ("Kritisch-exegetischer Kommentar"; Göttingen: Vandenhoeck und Ruprecht, 1924), pp. 429 ff., and in the literature listed therein.

[74] See above, p. 15.

[75] See above, n. 43.

inclined toward it.[76] Philo has not given the name "paraclete" to the Logos (nor to *nous*), but he has lent to the Logos the functions of the paraclete on earth. John could not have derived his concept from Philo, but the Philonic analogies support the conjecture that in Judaism there already existed, not only the idea of an interceding angel in heaven, but also the concept of an interceding angel sent to earth and carrying out his functions there. This figure may have blended with that of Elijah *redidivus*.

W. Bauer has pointed out still more compelling analogies in the Mandaean literature.[77] In this connection, I have in mind less the figure of Yawar (= helper) and more the nameless figure of the "great helper," the "messenger," the emissary who comes from on high and whom life has sent to the dying Šum bar Nu (= Sem) in order to teach him about the questions of life and death and to assure him of his salvation.[78] I have in mind, further, Yokabar-Kusta, whom Hibil, the guardian of the ages, appoints as "messenger," "helper," and "lord" over men of proved righteousness.[79] Finally, I have in mind the "exalted helper," "guardian," and "gentle comforter," whom the Great Life sends to the soul sighing over its enslavement by the Seven [planets].[80]

One must not identify these Mandaean paraclete-messengers with the Paraclete of the Johannine sayings. A few characteristic features of the latter—that he is the second emissary, that he supports the congregation in its witness concerning the chief emissary and that he also has a message for the world—are lacking in the Mandaean messenger, as far as I can see. Still, the Mandaean witnesses confirm our postulate that in the thought world in which the evangelist lived there existed the idea or expectation of a new emissary who, as the Paraclete, would help the faithful in their special needs. This idea was deposited in various Paraclete sayings which John made to refer to the Spirit and worked into his farewell discourses.[81]

---

[76] *De somniis* 1.86 (633). On further parallel functions of the Logos see J. Grill, *Untersuchungen über die Entstehung des vierten Evangeliums* (see above, n. 43), Vol. 1, pp. 135 f. Cf. further, E. F. Scott, *The Fourth Gospel: Its Purpose and Theology* (2d ed.; Edinburgh: T. & T. Clark, 1908), pp. 330 f.

[77] W. Bauer, *Das Johannesevangelium* (see above, n. 39), pp. 179 ff.

[78] M. Lidzbarski, *Das Johannesbuch der Mandäer* (Giessen: A. Töpelmann, 1915), pp. 60 f., 69 f.

[79] M. Lidzbarski (trans. and ed.), *Ginza der Schatz oder Das grosse Buch der Mändaer* ("Quellen der Religionsgeschichte," 13; Göttingen: Vandenhoeck und Ruprecht, 1925), pp. 319 f.

[80] *Ibid.*, pp. 328 f.

[81] The analogies which Grill cites (*Untersuchungen über die Entstehung des vierten Evangeliums,* pp. 331 f.) are not convincing.

JESUS AND THE SPIRIT
IN THE GOSPEL OF JOHN

ANYONE who comes from the Pauline epistles to the Synoptic Gospels is always surprised anew by the fact that so many concepts, benefits of salvation, and experiences central to Paul are either lacking or inconspicuous in the Synoptic accounts of the history and proclamation of Jesus. The Spirit is a striking example. According to Pauline teaching, Christ is the Lord of the Spirit, and each baptized and converted person also possesses the Spirit. Being in Christ and being in the Spirit are two almost identical descriptions of Christian existence and of the Christian experience of salvation.

Now, according to the Synoptic tradition, the belief that Jesus had the Spirit is quite securely grounded. But this is recorded in only two accounts, and they belong to different strata. Both accounts speak only of the *archē,* that is, of the beginning of his possession of the Spirit. One account is that of Jesus' baptism, first put into fixed form by Mark. The other, which Matthew and Luke present in divergent accounts, is that of the announcement by the angel that Jesus would be begotten by the Holy Spirit in the womb of his mother. It is striking that Jesus' possession of the Spirit is developed but little in the Synoptic tradition, that Jesus' words and deeds are only rarely derived from the Spirit, whom he possesses,[1] and that he himself seldom refers, in an explana-

[1] Cf. Mark 1:13 and parallel passages; Luke 4:14; Matt. 12:28 (Luke 11:20 differs ["the finger of God" rather than "the Spirit of God"]); Luke 10:21 (no parallels).

27

tory or admonitory way, to the Spirit whom he has and who reveals himself in Jesus' deeds.[2] In addition, even the promise of the Spirit to his disciples was embodied in only a single logion and in that instance appears in a strikingly restricted form as compared to the experience and teaching of Paul: only if the disciples must some day bear witness before a court will the Spirit come to them and speak through them.[3] These facts may be explained in different ways.

(1) One can *accept* the tradition as such and maintain, first, that Jesus spoke only infrequently of his possession of the Spirit, guarding it as a secret and testifying of it only when compelled to do so; and, second, that in reality he promised his disciples no general outpouring of the Spirit, but only momentary inspirations in times of need.

(2) One can attempt to *eliminate* the Spirit completely from the self-witness of Jesus and from the teaching he imparted to the disciples and try to explain the few references to the Spirit as the expressions of a Christianizing process [*Christianisierungsprozess*], that is, reading back into the accounts the Christian experience and the apostolic teaching concerning Christ (Goguel, Bultmann).

(3) Finally, one can conjecture an *abridgement* of the tradition, in the sense that later veneration of Christ was scandalized by the idea that Jesus might have performed his deeds and proclaimed his words of salvation "only" as a Pneumatic.[4] Be that as it may, these facts remain: the earliest tradition testifies clearly that Jesus was anointed with the Holy Spirit; it rarely permits him to act as the bearer of the Spirit in the power of the Spirit bestowed on him by God; and the early Christian pneumatology found expression in the Synoptic version of Jesus' promise of the Spirit only in a severely limited form.

With these observations in view, theological interest comes to attach to the question of how prominently the *pneuma* ["Spirit"] figures in the Christology and proclamation about the Christ in the Gospel of John.

---

[2] Cf. Matt. 12:31f. and parallel passages.

[3] Mark 13:11 and parallel passages; Luke 11:13 (secondary). Luke 24:49 and Acts 1:5 lie outside the sphere of the historical Jesus.

[4] On this point cf. H. Windisch, "Jesus und der Geist nach synoptischer Überlieferung," in *Studies in Early Christianity,* ed. S. J. Case (New York and London: The Century Company, 1928), pp. 207-36. The present study is a supplement to this article. Cf. also W. Michaelis, *Reich Gottes und Geist Gottes im Neuen Testament* (Basel: F. Reinhardt, 1931). M. Goguel, *Au seuil de l'Évangile: Jean-Baptiste* (Paris, 1928), pp. 192 ff. R. Bultmann, *Die Geschichte der synoptischen Tradition* (Göttingen: Vandenhoeck und Ruprecht, 1931), pp. 261 f.; trans. J. Marsh, *The History of the Synoptic Tradition* (Oxford: Blackwell, and New York: Harper, 1963), pp. 245-47.

If John is written essentially from a "post-Easter" standpoint, one could expect that Jesus the "Pneumatic" might be completely effaced here but that (a) either the promise of the Spirit might be more fully developed or (b) the bestowal of the Spirit might be incorporated into the earthly work of Jesus itself. These expectations are indeed more or less realized in the Fourth Gospel.

THE JOHANNINE EVIDENCE

To be specific, John first of all does not give any account of the begetting of Jesus by the Spirit. (Whether 1:13 alludes to it is doubtful.) On the other hand, he gives the story of the baptism only in an indirect version, namely, as a report by the Baptist, whereby, to be sure, a new motif comes to the fore: he on whom the Spirit will descend in order to indwell him permanently is who will baptize with Spirit (1:32-34).

In the second place, the evangelist has worked into the farewell discourses no fewer than five related sayings about the Paraclete, the Holy Spirit, which present with the greatest clarity the preconditions of his coming and his functions in the disciples and before the world.

In the third place, however, there are some conversations and sayings in which Jesus offers something like Spirit, i.e., actually performs the function of the one who baptizes with Spirit.

These propositions, however, must be elucidated in greater detail; moreover, they still do not exhaust the Johannine tradition about the Spirit in its entirety. One also sees immediately that the motifs which have just been pointed out are not altogether in harmony with one another and in fact clash with one another.

As we have already noted, John puts no emphasis on the birth of Jesus through the *pneuma*. That can be accounted for. First, the traditions of the Synoptic Gospels are not yet normative for him.[5] Second, the idea of generation by the *pneuma* conflicts with his doctrine of the pre-existent Logos, inasmuch as the former concept implies that the being, the man Jesus Christ, owes his existence to the Spirit of God, who in the nativity miraculously effected the generation in the virgin womb of Mary, and that Jesus Christ in this way became Son of God, having been begotten by the Spirit of God (Luke 1:35). Hence, John also would never have designated the incarnation of the

[5] Cf. H. Windisch, *Johannes und die Synoptiker* (Leipzig: J. C. Hinrichs, 1926), and "Die Absolutheit des Johannesevangeliums," *Zeitschrift für systematische Theologie,* 5 (1927/28), 3-54.

Logos as a "birth from God" [R.S.V.: "born . . . of God," John 1:13].
Already for this reason it is questionable whether the rebirth of believers in 1:13 should be placed in parallel with the miraculous birth
of the man Jesus; and that the variant reading in the singular[6] should
be regarded as the original one appears to be precluded.

It is all the more astonishing that John has not also eliminated
the tradition that the Spirit descended upon Jesus at his baptism,[7] and
that from this divine action John even derives a special honor and
function for Jesus: *the one who baptizes with Spirit*. The expression
ties in with the prophecy voiced by the Baptist in the Synoptics (Mark
1:8 and parallels). John has appropriated it because it lends itself to
use as a means of having Jesus' superiority over the Baptist declared
out of the Baptist's own mouth.

Nevertheless, this tradition in John looks like an alien entity. It
says too little and too much. It says too little, for, also according to
John, Jesus apparently became Son of God through the descent of the
Spirit upon him at his baptism;[8] John, too, is indeed acquainted with
the power of the Spirit to beget (see 3:3, 5), but his real opinion is
surely that Jesus as Son exists from eternity.[9] The tradition also says
too much, for it is questionable whether the idea that Jesus baptizes
with Spirit is realized in John either. For "to baptize with Spirit"
signifies passing on to another the Spirit which the one who does the
baptizing received at his own baptism. Through his baptism Jesus has
become the one who baptizes with Spirit. His work, his vocation, is
now to baptize with Spirit, just as the task of the Baptist was to baptize with water. However, John does not really present Jesus as one

---

[6] [Found in one Old Latin manuscript and several church fathers and rendered thus in *The Jerusalem Bible* (Garden City, N. Y.: Doubleday, 1966):
". . . him who was born . . . of God himself."—EDITOR.]

[7] Cf. the version of the baptismal voice found in Codex D (Luke 3:22), the
favorite codex of the esteemed octogenarian [James Rendel Harris] to whom
these studies are dedicated.

[8] Or we shall assume with M. Goguel, *Au seuil de l'Évangile*, pp. 159 ff.,
that John completely eliminated the baptism of Jesus or, indeed, represents
an older form of tradition, which did not yet know the baptism of Jesus by
John? In that case, the Baptist's reference to Jesus in John 1:33 would have
been realized in his first encounter with Jesus in John 1:29, without a baptism
ever having taken place. In fact, one can completely ignore the baptism of
Jesus if one restricts oneself to the Johannine text and refrains from every side
glance at the Synoptics. Then the specifically Johannine combination also remains intact, namely, that Jesus became the one who baptizes with Spirit
through his receiving and continuing to possess the Spirit.

[9] In John the baptism of Jesus is a vestige, not fully absorbed, of an adoptionist way of thinking.

who baptizes with Spirit. On the contrary, already in the gloss in 7:39, a promise by Jesus to believers refers expressly to reception of the Spirit only after Jesus' glorification, the present being designated as Spirit-less. This view is then abundantly confirmed in the Paraclete sayings, in which Jesus places the sending of the Spirit in prospect for the time after his departure. "Baptizing" with Spirit and "sending" of the Spirit are two totally different concepts: the first happens on earth from person to person, the other comes from heaven to earth.

Still, the predicate "he who baptizes with Spirit" (*ho baptizōn en pneumati*) as referring to the historical Jesus in no way stands in isolation in John. That the Spirit is perceptible in Jesus, is attested more than once: since he (God) gives the Spirit without measure,[10] Jesus speaks the words of God (according to John's testimony of him, 3:34); and Jesus himself characterizes his words as "spirit and life" (6:63). Accordingly, Jesus is designated as inspired, and his speaking is brought into relation to the equipping provided at his baptism. Thus one could call the effect Jesus exercised through the word a "baptism with Spirit," insofar as effect [*wirken*] implies effectiveness [*Einwirken*]. That, it is true, is not articulated.[11]

However, also in the account of the baptism of Jesus (3:22) one can discern the predicate "he who baptizes with the Spirit" if one combines the predicate with the baptismal saying in 3:5 (a "Christian" saying, of course). In the framework of the Nicodemus narrative, the idea lies close at hand, however, that such birth from water and Spirit is immediately possible if only man does not turn away from the offer. Also, the antithetical statements about flesh and Spirit (3:6-8) make sense only if they are already realized in the present. The combination of the predicate and the baptismal sayings is made difficult only by the fact that, according to 4:2, Jesus had his disciples do the work of baptizing;[12] thus the baptism of Jesus seems to sink to the level of a mere water ceremony.

[10] With W. Bauer, *Das Johannesevangelium* (3d ed.; Tübingen: J. C. B. Mohr, 1933), pp. 64 f., J. H. Bernard, *The Gospel According to St. John* ("International Critical Commentary"; Edinburgh: T. & T. Clark, 1928), Vol. 1, p. 125, and others, I regard God as the subject of the clause. In that case, here, too, a viewpoint strongly influenced by adoptionism is represented. Whoever regards Jesus as the subject, finds a witness here for a powerful pneumatic activity of Jesus on earth. That the Spirit is the subject (Zahn and others) is improbable, since the lack of an object (for "gives") would be too disturbing.

[11] Cf. F. Büchsel, *Der Geist Gottes im Neuen Testament* (Gütersloh: C. Bertelsmann, 1926), pp. 490 ff.

[12] Cf. Acts 10:47 ff.

One can find an allusion to baptizing with Spirit also in the conversation with the Samaritan woman, first, in the offer of living water (4:10 ff.), and then in the witness of the true worshipers, who worship God in the Spirit and in truth and who are now already at hand (4:21 ff.) To be sure, the identification of the new water with the Spirit is not made here, and it is not taught that the pneumatic worship is introduced by Jesus or made possible by him. Rather, its necessity is seen as a consequence of the pneumatic nature of God (the passage is a remarkable example of non-christocentric revelatory discourse). The first reservation noted, that the new water is not identified with the Spirit, is met, however, in view of 7:39, where a similar assertion is in fact related expressly to the Spirit. The interpretation connecting the water and the Spirit is therefore possible. Admittedly, according to the gloss [in 7:39] the Spirit's manifestation among the disciples took place only after the glorification of Jesus. However, this interpretation is artificial. In the saying in 7:37 f. two different concepts conflict with each other. According to one, Jesus, already in his earthly life, offered a gift of salvation which was susceptible of further miraculous efficacy —thus he has already appeared as the one who baptizes with Spirit. According to the other, he has only promised the gift, and the fulfillment is not experienced until after his death.[13]

Thus, the idea of Jesus as the one who baptizes with Spirit is a motif which finds expression in John several times. Naturally, it signifies a looking forward and is a new proof for the familiar thesis that John transferred the activities and experiences of the exalted Christ back into the life and work of Jesus. In these materials, too, there is Christianizing; in this instance, it consists in the introduction of the Christian experience of salvation into the story of Jesus.

The original idea, according to which the Spirit is experienced for the first time in the apostolic community as a gift of the Christ abiding in heaven, was preserved by John, however, in the saying in 7:39 and especially in the Paraclete sayings. In my essay on "The Five Johannine Paraclete Sayings"[14] I have tried to show that from the literary standpoint these pericopes are not original; rather, they are secondary insertions (probably by the evangelist himself) in the draft [*Entwurf*]

---

[13] The post-Easter standpoint of the evangelist is clearly betrayed in the "gloss."

[14] [Printed as the first essay in this Facet Book.] Cf. also H. Sasse, "Der Paraklet im Johannesevangelium," *Zeitschrift für die neutestamentliche Wissenschaft*, 24 (1925), 260 ff.; F. Büchsel, *Johannes und der hellenistiche Synkretismus* (Gütersloh: C. Bertelsmann, 1928), p. 101.

of his farewell discourses (in form as well as content they stand in clear contrast to their context).

If we compare with this the fact that the gloss in 7:39, which contains related ideas, is also secondary, then we see that in John the tradition—which corresponds to history and to the Synoptic tradition—of the post-Easter origin of the experience of the Spirit belongs to a subsequent redaction, while the actual, original idea of John is that of the one who baptizes with Spirit.

The tension between the two sets of tradition is clear and is expressed especially in the gloss in 7:39, where it is said that a solemn assurance which has unambiguous reference to the present moment is a promise relating to the time when Jesus will be absent. According to the text, Jesus, while still on earth, offers divine power, evidently since he possesses it himself; according to the gloss, he was unable to fulfill his promise before his "glorification." The conclusion to be drawn is that before his glorification he himself could not have been "one who baptizes with Spirit," for the formulation of the gloss has an absolute tone and allows of no compromise.[15]

However, John has yet a third tradition concerning the origin of the apostolic Spirit: according to 20:22 f., the Risen One breathed it upon his disciples. This view cannot be linked with either of the aforementioned views.[16] One can designate this action as a baptism with Spirit, it is true. However, in its framework, as an act of the Risen One, it is certainly no fulfillment of the Baptist's saying in 1:33, which implies, rather, an immediate exercise of this activity on the basis of the epiphany at the baptism. It is equally impossible to see in 20:22 ff. the fulfillment of the Paraclete prophecies. The Ascended One sends the Paraclete from heaven. He comes when Jesus is no longer present. He is his successor, his caliph on earth. The story stands completely on its own. Incidentally, this pericope, too, scarcely belongs to the original draft of John.[17]

It remains to be noted that according to 20:22 f. the gift of the Spirit expresses itself solely in the authority to forgive and to retain

[15] The observations of Büchsel, *Der Geist Gottes* (see above, note 11), p. 496, are therefore unsatisfactory.

[16] The report also "competes" with the Pentecost account in Acts; it represents, as it were, the "Johannine Pentecost." In John, Easter and Pentecost do indeed fall on *one* day.

[17] The appearance to Mary Magdalene is really intended as the only revelation of the Risen One. It is sufficient in itself, for it is equally valid for the disciples and immediately precedes the ascension in 20:17 f.

33

sins. It is, therefore, a specific mark of the apostle (cf. Mark 6:7 and parallel passages).

Thus three different views of the time of the reception of the Spirit may be seen in John. (1) According to the genuine Johannine teaching Jesus appeared on earth as the one who baptizes with Spirit. (2) According to a totally isolated legend of a post-resurrection appearance, Jesus, after his resurrection, bestowed the Spirit on his disciples by insufflation. (3) According to a form of teaching deposited in five sayings, and according to a remark of the evangelist provided in interpretation of them, the Spirit was "sent" as Paraclete to the disciples after the exaltation of Jesus.

COMPARISON WITH THE SYNOPTICS

If we now compare these facts in John with the situation in the first three Gospels, we find that the view concerning the one who baptizes with Spirit surely links itself with the saying of the Baptist in the Synoptics (Mark 1:8 and parallel passages). The Synoptics are distinguished from the Gospel of John in that they do not actually depict Jesus as the one who baptizes with Spirit. Nor is his casting out of devils a baptism with Spirit. We see how John, in the Christianizing of the Jesus tradition, goes further than any of the Synoptics.

The account of the impartation of the Spirit by the Risen One (point two above) reminds one of the mighty baptismal mandate of the Risen One in Matthew 28:19 f. It supplements it, to some degree, for if the disciples, too, are to baptize in the name of the Spirit, they must have been put in contact with the Spirit. Of course, nothing is mentioned in John 20:22 f. about baptizing. In Luke 24:48 f. the promise of the Spirit is only renewed; the evangelist, naturally, is working up to his story of Pentecost.

On the other hand, the Paraclete sayings (point three above) unmistakably link themselves with the promise of the Spirit in the Synoptics (Mark 13:11 and parallel passages). The connection is clearest in the third saying, John 15:26 f. In the second saying, the words "he will teach you all things" (*didaxei humas panta*) are in harmony, word for word, with the version in Luke 12:12. In the fourth saying, 16:8-11, the idea that the Spirit gives testimony before a court, before the representatives of the world, seems at least to form the basis of the view expressed in the saying.

In other respects, the specific content of the Synoptic saying is, admittedly, scarcely recognizable in the Johannine Paraclete sayings. First, the restriction of the promise to inspiration before the court is put aside: the Spirit has become the constant companion of the disciples (14:16); he helps the disciples to retain the figure of Jesus in their memories (and indeed in a glorious and more profound form) and supplements the teaching of Jesus (14:25 f.); he brings the disciples' knowledge of truth to completion (16:12-15). Second, in these Johannine sayings an altogether different figure, called the "Paraclete," who represents a kind of prophet or guardian angel on earth, is fused with the Spirit.

In all probability, John did not invent the Paraclete sayings. He came upon them in some form in his collections of revelatory sayings of Jesus, but he surely did not leave them unaltered. Above all, the interpretation of the "Paraclete" as referring to the Spirit probably derives from him. It should be emphasized that the sayings evince *no essential Pauline influence* and that the doctrine and experience of the Spirit found in the sayings is not congruent with Pauline teaching about the Spirit. The special functions of the Johannine Pneuma-Paraclete are little emphasized by Paul. One can cite from Paul parallels only to the first and the fourth Paraclete sayings: that the world does not see him and know him (John 14:17; cf. I Cor. 2:11) and that the Spirit convicts the unbelieving world of its sin (John 16:8; cf. I Cor. 14:24).[18] John conceives the whole phenomenon otherwise. Paul portrays especially the individual charisma and the action of the Spirit as the power of faith and of ethical discipline. John holds the view of a power of God working independently in and with the disciples, almost a divine person—to be compared with Jesus and replacing him —who appears on earth and has, above all, a particular "mission" over against the world. John also shows a strong didactic interest that diverges from Paul at this point. The disciples are to know exactly who the Spirit is, what his function is in the history of salvation, and what his relationship is to Jesus (Jesus on earth and Jesus in heaven). For John, too, then the chief function of the Spirit is teaching and witnessing, the vindication of Jesus, and the chastening of the world which remained unbelieving and sinful and fallen under judgment. He is the exponent of the Christian apologetic before the world and of the Christian reprimand of the world.

[18] On the other hand, the dualistic distinction "flesh and Spirit" in John 3:6ff. and the combination "spirit and life" in John 6:63 are reminiscent of Paul. However, the ideas about Jesus and the Spirit are not influenced by Paul, just as, conversely, the pneumatic Christology of Paul has no effect on John. H. J. Holtzmann, *Lehrbuch der neutestamentlichen Theologie,* Vol. 2 (2d ed. rev.; Tübingen: J. C. B. Mohr, 1911), pp. 513 ff., thinks otherwise.

Compared with the Synoptic tradition, John appears incomparably richer in the information he conveys about "Jesus and the Spirit," first, because in several places he has Jesus actually appear and work as the one who baptizes with Spirit; above all, because in five groups of sayings he has Jesus portray in detail the sending and the activity of the Spirit; and, finally, because he even reports explicitly the equipping of the disciples with the Spirit. But the actual demonstration of Jesus as one "inspired" is missing in John. He can afford to include it even less than the Synoptics can. The Johannine Christ receives his instructions directly from the Father: in what he "sees" and "hears" and in what the Father "shows" to him the Spirit is scarcely to be regarded as a mediator. In the quite singular saying in 1:51, the angels are the ones who convey to him the instructions of the Father.[19] Otherwise, in John's Gospel Jesus has no visions of any kind. The profound emotions which Jesus experienced "in his spirit" at the grave of Lazarus (11:33) and at the Last Supper (13:21) are not the excitations of the Pneumatic. The Johannine Jesus, in accord with old tradition, is, to be sure, also introduced as a man on whom the Spirit has descended,[20] but his real manifestation is as the Son of God and Son of man descended from heaven. And as Son of the Father he does not "have" the Spirit—not to mention that the Spirit "might have him"—rather, the Spirit is at his disposal. While the Synoptics still clearly teach the dependence of Jesus on the Spirit (especially in the baptism story) and even the superiority of the Spirit to Jesus (in the saying on blasphemy in Matt. 12:31 f.), John stresses very emphatically the subordination of the Spirit to Jesus: with respect to the divine duality of Father and Son he is the third person and the subordinate (16:14 f.). If in the Synoptics the Trinity is still referred to preponderantly as

God—Spirit—Jesus

or

God—Spirit—Son of man,

in John (as already in Matt. 28:18) the schema is

Father—Son—Spirit.

Or, in a better representation, the Synoptic Triad,

God—Spirit

Jesus,

[19] Cf. my article: "Angelophanien um den Menschensohn auf Erden," *Zeitschrift für die neutestamentliche Wissenschaft*, 30 (1931), 215-33, and 31 (1932), 199-204.

[20] Cf. with this the Old Testament prefiguration in Isa. 61:1 f., which has had influence here and is expressly cited in Luke 4:18 f.

stands in contrast to the Johannine Triad,

Father—Son
Spirit.

The later, more developed Christology allotted to the Son, but also to the Spirit, the place "befitting" each alongside God the Father.

Finally, as far as the disciples' possession of the Spirit is concerned, John, too, confirms the old tradition that during the earthly life of Jesus the disciples did not yet have the Spirit and that Jesus placed the Spirit in prospect only for the time after his exaltation. John even has a doctrine of the necessity of this course of events (7:39; 16:7). Because he had not yet been glorified, Jesus could not yet bestow the Spirit, and the Spirit could not and must not work alongside Jesus, simultaneously with him on earth. The latter is a very remarkable idea that is not explained any further. Therefore, in an episode in the resurrection narrative, the bestowal of the Spirit through the risen Jesus is expressly reported—however, as already noted, this Spirit is not the Paraclete.

As we saw, however, John has broken through this tradition, too, when he has Jesus speak and act already on earth as the one who baptizes with Spirit. However, this view, in which the post-Easter Jesus is so rightly fused with the historical Jesus, shines through only in the first chapters of the Fourth Gospel. And this view is not a complete novelty within the Gospel tradition. For when it is stated in the Synoptic commissioning address that he gave the disciples "authority" over the unclean spirits (Mark 6:7; Matt. 10:1; in Luke 9:1 even more clearly: he gave them "power and authority," etc.), this means, according to the saying in Matthew 12:28 and as generally interpreted from the history-of-religions standpoint, that, as a Pneumatic, Jesus passes on to his disciples something of his possession of the *pneuma*. By virtue of his possession of the Spirit he makes them Pneumatics too, in this case, pneumatic exorcists and miracle healers (cf. further Luke 10:19). The Synoptic equipping of the disciples for their apostolic journey is a parallel to the Johannine scene in 20:22 f. In this case, therefore, it is the Synoptic tradition which manifestly transfers back into the earthly life of Jesus an action of the Risen One. To look at it in another way, the Johannine view of Jesus as the one who baptizes with Spirit has already found an illustration in the Synoptics too—and in fact in a tradition which John has eliminated.

Thus here, too, the result is that the distinctions between the Synoptics (as a whole) and John are not absolute. The process of Christianizing the events and the words is already underway in the Synoptics. And while John has carried out this process radically in the shaping of his accounts and discourses, alongside he has also preserved still older, "pre-Christian" tradition. Thus inconsistencies result which are explicable in view of the diversity in the tradition at his disposal and in view of his many-sided theological concerns.

We close with some remarks of a more theological nature.

Out of the manifold parallel and competing traditions of the four evangelists on "Jesus and the Spirit," two fundamental views requiring dogmatic development and evaluation stand out in bold relief: (1) the Spirit is a gift of the ascended Jesus, a gift that lays the foundation of the church, or the Spirit is a gift of God to the disciples who are left bereft of their Lord; and (2) the historical Jesus was already a bearer of the Spirit and one who baptized with Spirit. It is not so easy to bring both ideas into an inner unity, but both contain truth for the believer. A person will lay more stress now on the one, now on the other. The second view is of significance insofar as it is a point of departure, derived from the tradition, for a true "Christology." It embraces the majesty and work of Jesus as that of the Christ. If one steeps oneself in it, the historical Christ develops directly into the suprahistorical Christ. As bearer of the Spirit and the one who baptized with Spirit, Jesus of Nazareth walked upon the earth. As bearer of the Spirit, as lord of spirits, and as the one who baptizes with Spirit, he strides through the history of his church, judging and blessing, and he builds the kingdom of God, which, according to his promise, shall come.

For Further Reading

(Abbreviations: *ThR = Theologische Rundschau;* "UNT" = "Untersuchungen zum Neuen Testament," ed. H. Windisch; *ZNW = Zeitschrift für die neutestamentliche Wissenschaft.*)

About Hans Windisch:

BEIJER, ERIK. "Hans Windisch und seine Bedeutung für die neutestamentliche Wissenschaft," *ZNW*, 48 (1957), 22-49. This study was written for the Festschrift for Anton Fridrichsen (*Svensk exegetisk Årsbok*, 17) and appeared originally, in Swedish, in the next edition of the *Årsbok*, 18-19 (1953/54), 109-39, under the title "Hans Windisch som nytestamentlig forskare"; German translation by E. Schreiter and W. Klein. It presents a brief sketch of Windisch's life, his work on Jesus and Paul and John, and his general history-of-religions approach.

PRÜMM, KARL, S.J. "Zur Früh- und Spätform der Religionsgeschichtlichen Christusdeutung von H. Windisch," *Biblica*, 42 (1961), 391-422, and 43 (1962), 22-56. A Jesuit scholar, who himself has dealt extensively with *Religionsgeschichte* and has written a commentary on II Corinthians, analyzes Windisch's treatment of Jesus, especially on the basis of II Corinthians 8:9, as a "divine" (*theios*) personage. The second part of his treatment takes up Windisch's contention that Jesus was a prophet and *Pneumatiker*.

DELLING, GERHARD. "In Memoriam Hans Windisch," *Theologische Literaturzeitung*, 81 (1956), col. 499. (On the seventy-fifth anniversary of the birth of Windisch.) A full bibliography, including book reviews, is given by M. J. Fiedler, cols. 500-10.

By Hans Windisch:

IN ENGLISH TRANSLATION

The Meaning of the Sermon on the Mount: a Contribution to the Historical Understanding of the Gospels and to the Problem of Their True Exegesis. Translated from the revised German edition of 1937 by S. MacLean Gilmour. Philadelphia: Westminster, 1951. A brief introduction about Windisch is included. The book states well his general view of the study of the gospels and of Jesus.

Articles in the *Theologisches Wörterbuch zum Neuen Testament* (ed. Gerhard Kittel; Stuttgart: Kohlhammer); English translation by G. W. Bromiley, *Theological Dictionary of the New Testament* (Grand Rapids: Eerdmans):

Vol. I (1933); Eng. trans., I (1964)—*askeō*, "exert oneself, take pains, practice asceticism," pp. 492-94 (Eng. trans., pp. 494-96); *aspazomai*, etc., "greet, greeting," pp. 494-500 (Eng. trans., pp. 496-502); *barbaros*, "barbarian," pp. 544-51 (Eng. trans., pp. 546-53).

Vol. II (1935); Eng. trans., II (1964)—*Hellēn*, etc., "Greek," pp. 501-14 (Eng. trans., 504-16); *zumē*, "leaven," pp. 904-8 (Eng. trans., pp. 902-6).

Vol. III (1938); Eng. trans., III (1965)—*kapēleuo*, "peddle," pp. 606-9 (Eng. trans., pp. 603-5).

"The Case against the Tradition" [against the traditional view that Luke wrote Acts], in *The Beginnings of Christianity*. Edited by F. J. Foakes Jackson and K. Lake. London: Macmillan. Vol. 2 (1922). Pp. 298-348.

"Literature on the New Testament in Germany, Austria, Switzerland, Holland, and the Scandinavian Countries 1914-1920," *Harvard Theological Review*, 15 (1922), 115-26.

"Literature on the New Testament in Germany, Holland, and the Scandinavian Countries 1921-24 (with the aid of A. Fridrichsen)," *Harvard Theological Review*, 19 (1926), 1-114.

PUBLISHED IN GERMAN OR DUTCH

(Arranged chronologically, except for encyclopedia articles which appeared over several years and articles on the Johannine literature, which are listed separately at the end.)

1906 *Die Theodizee des christlichen Apologeten Justin*. Leipzig: C. Kreysing, 1906. (Dissertation in the Philosophical Faculty, Leipzig.)

"Das Evangelium des Basilides," *ZNW*, 7 (1906), 236-47.

1908 *Taufe und Sünde im ältesten Christentum bis auf Origenes: Ein Beitrag zur altchristlichen Dogmengeschichte*. Tübingen: J. C. B. Mohr. (Incorporates his dissertation and *Habilitationsschrift* in the Theological Faculty at Leipzig.)

1909 *Die Frömmigkeit Philos und ihre Bedeutung für das Christentum. Eine religionsgeschichtliche Studie*. Leipzig: J. C. Hinrichs.

Der messianische Krieg und das Urchristentum. Tübingen: J. C. B. Mohr.

"Jesus und Paulus," *Die Christliche Welt*, 23 (1909), cols. 914-19, 942-49, 962-65.

1910 "Der geschichtliche Jesus," *ThR*, 13 (1910), 163-82.

1911 *Die katholischen Briefe.* ("Handbuch zum Neuen Testament," 15.) Tübingen: J. C. B. Mohr, 1911; 2d ed. revised, 1930.

"Die Dauer der öffentlichen Wirksamkeit Jesu nach den vier Evangelisten," *ZNW,* 12 (1911), 141-75. (Issue in honor of Harnack's sixtieth birthday.)

(With H. Jordan) "Ein Briefwechsel über die Jesusfrage der Gegenwart," *Die Christliche Welt,* 25 (1911), cols. 967-70, 986-93, 1013-18.

1913 *Der Hebräerbrief.* ("Handbuch zum Neuen Testament," 14.) Tübingen: J. C. B. Mohr, 1913; 2d ed. revised, 1931.

1914 "Der Untergang Jerusalems (anno 70) im Urteil der Christen und Juden," *Theologisch Tijdschrift,* 48 (1914), 519-50.

"Die göttliche Weisheit der Juden und die paulinische Christologie," *Neutestamentliche Studien für Georg Heinrici. . . .* ("UNT," 6.) Leipzig: J. C. Hinrichs. Pp. 220-34.

1917 "Kleine Beiträge zur evangelischen Überlieferung," *ZNW,* 18 (1917/18), 73-83.

"Das Erlebnis des Sünders in den Evangelien," *Zeitschrift für Theologie und Kirche,* 27 (1917), 292-313. (Festgabe für Wilhelm Hermann zu seinem 70. Geburtstag. . . .) Edited by M. Rade and H. Stephan. Tübingen: J. C. B. Mohr.

1918 "Urchristentum und Hermesmystik," *Theologisch Tijdschrift,* 52 (1918), 186-240.

1920 *Der Barnabasbrief.* ("Handbuch zum Neuen Testament," Supplementary Volume 3.) Tübingen: J. C. B. Mohr.

1921 "Das Christentum des zweiten Clemensbrief," in *Harnack-Ehrung: Beiträge zur Kirchengeschichte ihrem Lehrer Adolf von Harnack . . . (7 Mai 1921) dargebracht. . . .* Leipzig: J. C. Hinrichs. Pp. 119-34.

"Englisch-amerikanische Literatur zum Neuen Testament in den Jahren 1914-20," *ZNW,* 20 (1921), 69-90 and 147-65.

1924 *Der zweite Korintherbrief.* ("Kritisch-exegetischer Kommentar über das Neuen Testament," 6 [Meyer series].) 9th ed. Göttingen: Vandenhoeck & Ruprecht, 1924.

De tegenwoordige stand van het Christusprobleem. Assen, Holland: van Gorcum.

"Das Problem des paulinischen Imperativs," *ZNW,* 23 (1924), 265-81. (A reply to Rudolf Bultmann, "Das Problem der Ethik bei Paulus," pp. 123-40 in the same journal.)

1925 "Friedensbringer—Gottessöhne. Eine religionsgeschichtliche Interpretation der 7. Seligpreisung," *ZNW,* 24 (1925), 240-60.

1926 "Julius Cassianus und die Clemenshomilie (II Clemens)," *ZNW,* 25 (1926), 258-62.

1927 "Die Verstockungsidee in Mc 4,12 und das kausale *hina* der späteren Koine," *ZNW,* 26 (1927), 203-9.

1928 "Jesus und der Geist nach synoptischer Überlieferung," in *Studies in Early Christianity* (Presented to Frank Chamberlin Porter and Benjamin W. Bacon). Edited by Shirley Jackson Case. New York and London: The Century Company, 1928. Pp. 207-36. Discussed in C. K. Barrett, *The Holy Spirit,* cited below.

"Die Sprüche vom Eingehen in das Reiche Gottes," *ZNW,* 27 (1928), 163-92.

1929 *Der Sinn der Bergpredigt.* ("UNT," 16.) 2d ed. Leipzig: J. C. Hinrichs, 1937. English translation, *The Meaning of the Sermon on the Mount,* listed above.

Die Orakel des Hystaspes. Verhandelingen der Koninklijke Akademie van Wetenschappen te Amsterdam. Afdeeling Letterkunde, nieuwe Reeks, deel xxviii, No. 3. Amsterdam: Koninklijke Akademie van Wetenschappen, 1929. (Windisch also wrote an article on this "oracle" in the encyclopedia *RGG,* listed below.)

"Zum Problem der Kindertaufe im Urchristentum," *ZNW,* 28 (1929), 118-42.

"Das Problem der Geschichtlichkeit Jesu: Die ausserchristlichen Zeugnisse," *ThR,* N.F. 1 (1929), 266-88.

1930 "Das Problem der Geschichtlichkeit Jesu. Die Christus-Mythe," *ThR,* N.F. 2 (1930), 207-52.

1931 *Imperium und Evangelium im Neuen Testament.* Kiel: Lipsius & Tischer.

1932 "Die Christusepiphanie vor Damaskus (Act 9,22 und 26) und ihre religionsgeschichtlichen Parallelen," *ZNW,* 31 (1932), 1-23.

1933 "Die Notiz über Tract und Speise des Täufers Johannes und ihre Entsprechungen in der Jesusüberlieferung," *ZNW,* 32 (1933), 65-87.

1934 *Paulus und Christus. Ein biblisch-religionsgeschichlicher Vergleich.* ("UNT," 24.) Leipzig: J. C. Hinrichs.

1935 "Paulus und Jesus," *Theologische Studien und Kritiken,* 106 (1934/35), 432-68. (Windisch's last lectures of October 14-15, 1935, at Halle.)

Paulus und das Judentum. Stuttgart: Kohlhammer.

"Zum Corpus Hellenisticum," *ZNW,* 34 (1935), 124-25.

"Zur Christologie der Pastoralbriefe," *ZNW,* 34 (1935), 213-38.

ENCYCLOPEDIA ARTICLES

1909-13 *Die Religion in Geschichte und Gegenwart.* Edited by F. M. Schiele. 1st ed. Tübingen: J. C. B. Mohr. Many minor articles.

1913   *Realencyklopädie für protestantische Theologie und Kirche.* 3d ed., Supplementary Volumes 23 and 24. Edited by A. Hauck. Leipzig: J. C. Hinrichs, 1913. Windisch wrote supplements, often of a bibliographical nature, to the articles on "Jakobusbrief," "Jesus Christ," "Josephus," "Lukas," and "Pharisäer und Sadducäer." The English translation, *The New Schaff-Herzog Encyclopedia of Religious Knowledge* (1908-1912), does not include these supplementary materials.

1927-31   *Die Religion in Geschichte und Gegenwart.* Edited by H. Gunkel and L. Zscharnack. 2d ed. Tübingen: J. C. B. Mohr. Windisch wrote articles on "Alexander von Abonuteichos," "Euthalius," "Florilegien," "Glaube im NT," "Herodes und seine Nachfolger," "Hystaspes," "Johannesapokalypse," "Isebel," "Leiden im NT," "Libanius," "Lublinski, Samuel," "Lucian von Samosata," "Maurenbrecher, Max," "Neupythagoräer," and "Numenius."

ON THE FOURTH GOSPEL

1909   "Der Apokalyptiker Johannes als Begründer des neutestamentlichen Kanons," *ZNW,* 10 (1909), 148-74.

1913   "Die johanneischen Weinregel. (Joh. 2,10)," *ZNW,* 14 (1913), 248-57.

1923   "Der johanneische Erzählungsstil," *EUCHARISTERION. Studien zur Religion und Literatur des Alten und Neuen Testaments, Hermann Gunkel . . . dargebracht.* Edited by H. Schmidt. ("Forschungen zur Religion und Literatur des Alten und Neuen Testaments," N.F. 19, 1-2.) Göttingen: Vandenhoeck & Ruprecht, 1923. Vol. 2, pp. 147-213.

1925   "Over strekking en echtheid der Lazarus-parabel," *Nieuw theologisch Tijdschrift,* 14 (1925), 343-60.

1926   *Johannes und die Synoptiker. Wollte der vierte Evangelist die älteren Evangelien ergänzen oder ersetzen?* ("UNT," 12.) Leipzig: J. C. Hinrichs. Cf. S. Mender, "Zum Problem 'Johannes und die Synoptiker,'" *New Testament Studies,* 4 (1957-58), 282-307.

1927   "Die Absolutheit des Johannesevangeliums," *Zeitschrift für systematische Theologie,* 5 (1927/28), 3-54.
"Die fünf johanneischen Parakletsprüche," in *Festgabe für Adolf Jülicher zum 70. Geburtstag 26 Januar 1927.* Tübingen: J. C. B. Mohr. Pp. 110-37.

1931   "Angelophanien um den Menschensohn auf Erden. Ein Kommentar zu Joh 1,51," *ZNW,* 30 (1931), 215-33.

1932   "Joh 1,15 und die Auferstehung Jesu. Ein Nachtrag zu dem Aufsatz: Angelophanien," etc., *ZNW,* 31 (1932), 199-204.

1933 "Jesus und der Geist im Johannesevangelium," in *Amicitiae Corolla: A Volume of Essays Presented to James Rendel Harris, D. Litt. on the Occasion of His Eightieth Birthday.* Edited by H. G. Wood. London: University of London Press. Pp. 303-18.

1937 "Das vierte Evangelium und Johannes. Ein Beitrag zur Frage nach dem Selbstzeugnis des Johannesevangeliums," *Theologische Blätter,* 16 (1937), 144-52.

About the Paraclete:

BARRETT, C. K. *The Holy Spirit and the Gospel Tradition.* London: SPCK, 1947; reprinted, 1966. See pp. 3-4 for a summary on Windisch's view of Jesus as a *Pneumatiker.*

————. "The Holy Spirit in the Fourth Gospel," *Journal of Theological Studies,* N.S. 1 (1950), 1-15.

BEHM, J. *paraklētos* in Kittel's *Theologisches Wörterbuch.* Stuttgart: Kohlhammer. Vol. 5 (1954). Pp. 798-812.

BETZ, OTTO. *Der Paraklet. Fürsprecher im häretischen Spätjudentum, im Johannes-Evangelium und in neu gefundenen gnostischen Schriften.* ("Arbeiten zur Geschichte des Spätjudentums und Urchristentums," 2.) Leiden: Brill, 1963. A survey of recent work on the Paraclete, including the views of Windisch, plus consideration of Qumran and recently found gnostic documents.

BORNKAMM, GÜNTHER. "Der Paraklet im Johannesevangelium," in *Festschrift Rudolf Bultmann zum 65. Geburtstag überreicht.* Stuttgart: Kohlhammer, 1949. Pp. 12-35.

BROWN, RAYMOND. "The Paraclete in the Fourth Gospel," *New Testament Studies,* 13 (1966-67), 113-32. The most recent thorough survey in English. Readers should also consult, when it appears, the discussion of the pertinent Johannine passages in volume two of Brown's commentary treatment in the "Anchor Bible" on John. This article provides further bibliography in its notes, a survey of current opinions, and Brown's own position. See also *The Gospel according to John, I-XII* ("Anchor Bible," 29; New York: Doubleday, 1966), pp. xxvi-xxviii.

DAVIES, J. G. "The Primary Meaning of PARAKLETOS," *Journal of Theological Studies,* N.S. 4 (1953), 35-38.

FIROR, W. M. "Fulfillment of the Promise: The Holy Spirit and the Christian Life," *Interpretation,* 7 (1953), 299-314.

HOWARD, W. F. *Christianity according to St. John.* Philadelphia: Westminster, 1946. On Windisch, see pp. 72-74.

————. *The Fourth Gospel in Recent Criticism and Interpretation.* Revised by C. K. Barrett. 4th ed. London: Epworth, 1955. Pp. 71-74, 135-36 provide the best English summary on Windisch's work.

JOHANSSON, NILS. *Parakletoi: Vorstellungen von Fürspecher für die Menschen vor Gott in der alttestamentlichen Religion, im Spätjudentum und Urchristentum.* Lund: Gleerup, 1940.

JOHNSTON, GEORGE. " 'Spirit' and 'Holy Spirit' in the Qumran Literature," in *New Testament Sidelights: Essays in Honor of Alexander Converse Purdy.* Edited by Harvey K. McArthur. Hartford: Hartford Seminary Foundation Press, 1960. Pp. 27-42.

LOCHER, GOTTFRIED W. "Der Geist als Paraklet: Eine exegetisch-dogmatische Besinnung," *Evangelische Theologie,* 26 (1966), 565-79.

LOFTHOUSE, W. F. "The Holy Spirit in the Acts and the Fourth Gospel," *The Expository Times,* 52 (1940-41), 334-36.

MICHAELIS, W. "Zur Herkunft des johanneischen Paraklet-Titels," *Coniectanea Neotestamentica,* 11 (1947), 147-62. (Festschrift for Anton Fridrichsen.)

MOWINCKEL, SIGMUND. "Die Vorstellungen des Späjudentums vom heiligen Geist als Fürsprecher und der johanneische Paraklet," *ZNW,* 32 (1933), 97-130.

MUSSNER, F. "Die johanneische Parakletsprüche und die apostolische Tradition," *Biblische Zeitschrift,* 5 (1961), 56-70.

SCHLIER, HEINRICH. "Zum Begriff des Geistes nach dem Johannesevangelium," in *Neutestamentliche Aufsätze: Festschrift für Prof. Josef Schmid zum 70. Geburtstag.* Edited by J. Blinzler, O. Kuss, and F. Mussner. Regensburg: Pustet, 1963. Pp. 233-39. Reprinted in Schlier's *Besinnungen auf das Neue Testament: Exegetische Aufsätze und Vorträge II.* Freiburg: Herder, 1964. Pp. 264-71.

SCHWEIZER, EDUARD. *Spirit of God,* "Bible Key Words from Gerhard Kittel's *Theologisches Wörterbuch zum Neuen Testament,*" 9. Translated by A. E. Harvey. London A. & C. Black, 1960. Pp. 95-97 deal with John.

SNAITH, NORMAN H. "The Meaning of 'The Paraclete,' " *The Expository Times,* 57 (1945-46), 47-50.

Facet Books Already Published

19. *The Psalms: A Form-Critical Introduction*
   by Hermann Gunkel (translated by Thomas M. Horner). 1967

20. *The Spirit-Paraclete in the Fourth Gospel*
   by Hans Windisch (translated by James W. Cox). 1968

SOCIAL ETHICS SERIES:

1. *Our Calling*
   by Einar Billing (translated by Conrad Bergendoff). 1965

2. *The World Situation*
   by Paul Tillich. 1965

3. *Politics as a Vocation*
   by Max Weber (translated by H. H. Gerth and C. Wright
   Mills). 1965

4. *Christianity in a Divided Europe*
   by Hanns Lilje. 1965

5. *The Bible and Social Ethics*
   by Hendrik Kraemer. 1965

6. *Christ and the New Humanity*
   by C. H. Dodd. 1965

7. *What Christians Stand For in the Secular World*
   by William Temple. 1965

8. *Legal Responsibility and Moral Responsibility*
   by Walter Moberly. 1965

9. *The Divine Command: A New Perspective on Law and Gospel*
   by Paul Althaus (translated by Franklin Sherman). 1966

10. *The Road to Peace*
   by John C. Bennett, Kenneth Johnstone, C. F. von Weizsäcker,
   Michael Wright. 1966

11. *The Idea of a Natural Order: With an Essay on Modern
   Asceticism*
   by V. A. Demant. 1966

12. *Kerygma, Eschatology, and Social Ethics*
   by Amos N. Wilder. 1966

13. *Affluence and the Christian*
   by Hendrik van Oyen (translated by Frank Clarke). 1966

14. *Luther's Doctrine of the Two Kingdoms*
   by Heinrich Bornkamm (translated by Karl H. Hertz). 1966

15. *Christian Decision in a Nuclear Age*
   by T. R. Milford. 1967

16. *Law and Gospel*
   by Werner Elert (translated by Edward H. Schroeder). 1967

17. *On Marriage*
   by Karl Barth (translated by A. T. Mackay *et al.*). 1968

Body, 10 on 11 Garamond
Display, Garamond
Paper, White Spring Grove E. F.